The Little Book of **Drawing** SECRETS

A World of Practical Art in Your Pocket

Anne Corless

DAVID & CHARLES
—PUBLISHING—

www.davidandcharles.com

Contents

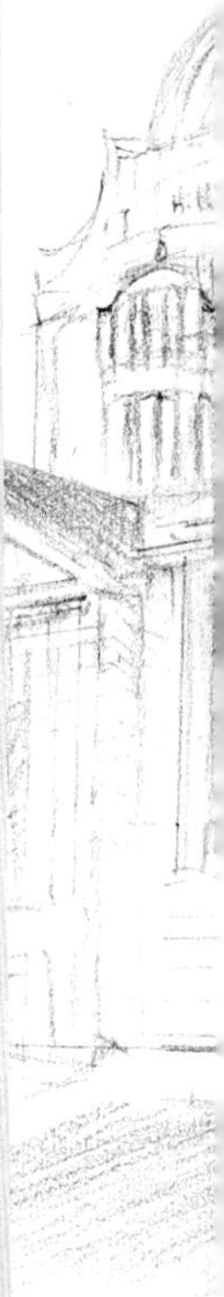

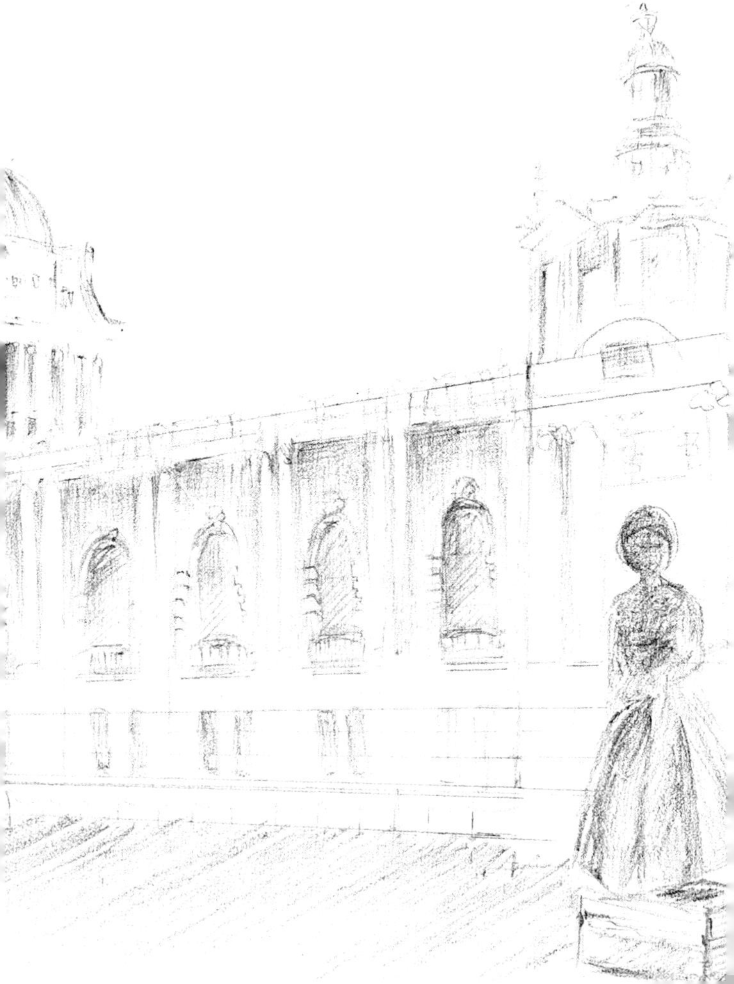

CHAPTER 1

Essential Materials

An Artist's Toolkit

It is easier to make creative decisions when you have a good understanding of how art materials work together. Different materials really do give different results, and an important part of my creative practice is spending time exploring and researching. However, a simple drawing only requires a pencil, drawing paper, and an eraser.

Making the Right Choice

Choose your materials to suit each project. Sketching, preparatory drawings, and thumbnails can be done in a sketchbook or on loose sheets of drawing paper. Final artwork that is intended to last is best done on archival-quality paper. Manufacturers state expected lengths of time a surface and other art materials will remain in good condition, depending on factors such as other materials used and if they are kept away from heat, sunlight, and damp. Manufacturers also have guides on the lightfast ratings of colored pencils, paints, and dyes indicating how long the color will last when exposed to light, before fading.

Working with a range of media and exploring different ways of working helps to improve confidence and control in mark making. Learn to recognize the "feel" of using different media.

Drawing is convenient, portable, and requires little preparation, especially when traveling. I first visited the Trevi Fountain in Rome as a child and I must have tossed a coin into the fountain, as the legend goes, as I returned years later. I chose a simple sketchbook, pencil, and eraser so that I could focus on a contour drawing. Using a heavier line weight to indicate shadow areas, I observed highlights, texture, and detail. I drew one of the Tritons (a merman) leading a winged hippocampus (a mythical sea horse), representing the wild sea. Drawing this brought back memories of my childhood trip.

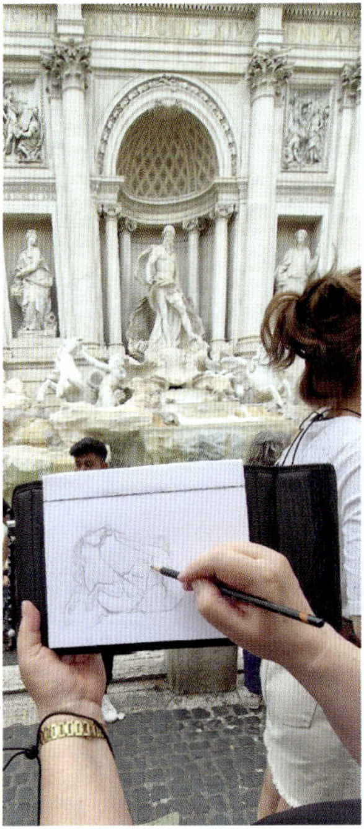

Use your "go-to" art materials to achieve reliable results. Explore using other materials when there is less time pressure.

Art Surfaces

Different art surfaces are available for different art materials, so choose carefully.

ART PAPER

This is available as single sheets, pads, and on rolls. Sketchbooks come in all shapes and sizes. The color of "white" paper can vary from bright white, which may be due to optical brighteners used in the paper-making process, to cream. Paper can be made by machine molds or by hand. If artwork needs to be long lasting, then it is good practice to use 100 percent cotton paper, which is both acid-free and lignin-free.

Paper comes in a range of textures. Hot pressed or smooth paper is suitable for highly detailed line work. Rough paper has more tooth (undulating "peaks" and "valleys" that create texture). Rough paper allows more of the medium to adhere to the surface, giving greater depth of tone, but it may be difficult to achieve fine detail. Cold pressed (not hot pressed or NOT) paper sits between hot pressed and rough and is a good compromise.

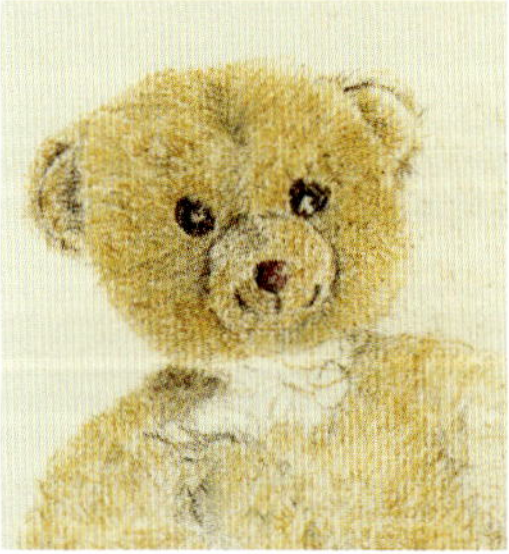

Most art papers have sizing, a glue-type substance that controls the absorption of water. Blotting paper is unsized.

OTHER SURFACES

- Cartridge paper is often used for preliminary drawings and sketches but you may not be able to achieve the same full range of marks, from light to dark, that a paper with more tooth will allow.
- Bristol board is smooth and come as vellum, semi-smooth, smooth, and plate (very smooth) and are 2-, 3-, or 4-ply (layers of paper pasted together).
- Illustration or art board is sheets of drawing paper stuck to one or both sides of a lightweight board.
- Pastel or charcoal paper and mixed media paper work well with their intended media. For instance, pastel and charcoal papers have more tooth for the mediums to adhere to. Mixed media paper resists bleeding, such as when using felt tip pens.
- Toned or colored paper offers a mid-tone to draw lighter and darker marks on.

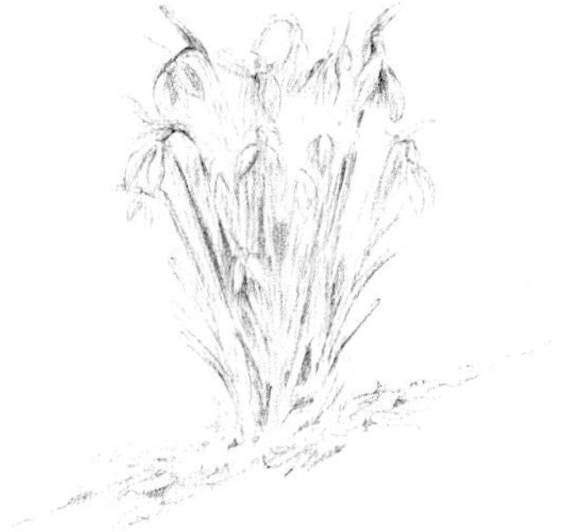

If the manufacturer's name is embossed or watermarked on one side of the paper, that is usually the top or "felt" side. The opposite side will show marks from the wire or mold it was held on. It's a personal choice which side you use.

SKETCHBOOKS

A sketchbook is your "go-to" place to collect and store visual information. It is the place to play with lines, to doodle, to scribble, and to come up with design ideas. An empty sheet of high-quality paper might stop you in your creative tracks but start doodling on sketch paper and ideas should flow. If you are sketching on a loose sheet of paper, you can always store it in your sketchbook.

Most importantly, remember that all your creative flair, your ideas, jottings, drawings, and studies in your sketchbooks are really just for you—for reference, for inspiration, and to help you find some space for creativity in your life.

Sketching regularly helps build confidence in drawing. It became part of my creative practice when I realized that I needed to draw regularly to keep my hand-eye coordination skills topped up. I also do preparatory drawings and thumbnails for nearly all my final artwork projects.

So, how do you choose a sketchbook?

Spiral-bound sketchbooks open flat but there is a gap between the two pages when laid flat. Some bound sketchbooks also lie flat but media can collect in the crease. Sketchbooks with perforated pages are ideal for removing pages, some even have storage pockets in them. Pocket-sized sketchbooks are fun to use when traveling. A sketchbook does not have to be neat and tidy but it works best if you can keep track of your drawings with notes as you work.

Sketching on different types of paper can help you develop a feel for sketching freely. It can also challenge you to consider how you are drawing, and encourage an exploration of mark making.

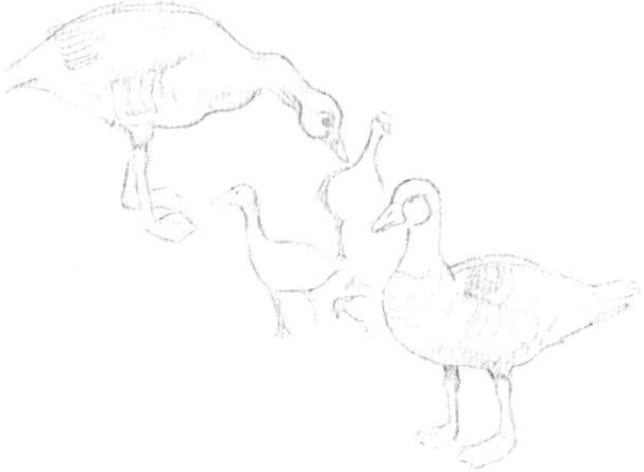

These geese were sketched on light gray Derwent toned paper. It shows how using pencil gives dark tones, white pencil gives highlights, and the paper is a mid-tone.

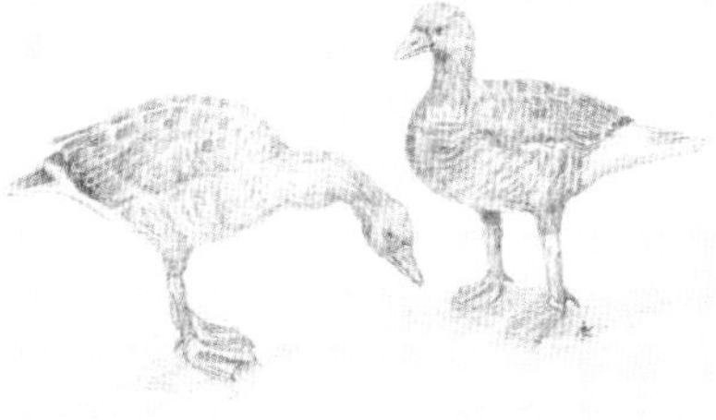

Graphite

Natural graphite is pure carbon mineral from the earth. The name graphite is derived from the Greek word "*grapho*" (meaning write). Art manufacturers mix graphite with different amounts of clay or other fillers and encase the pencil with wood. The shapes of pencil casings can vary from round to hexagonal.

A graphite pencil is easy to hold in different ways, to use on its point for detail or on its side to make expressive marks, or to apply value. With use, the pencil will need frequent sharpening and as it becomes shorter, you will notice the weight and feel of the pencil will change.

Propelling (clutch, lead holder, mechanical, or technical) pencils hold the lead in place within the pencil until released by a mechanism, making the lead shorter or longer. The advantage is a uniform weight so the feel of the pencil does not change. Each size of lead has a specific sized holder.

Note that lead has never been part of the writing material of a pencil but in the past was used in paint to cover pencils.

Graphite pencils are graded and make different marks.

- H equates to hard graphite pencils ranging from 9H, which is the hardest and makes the lightest marks, to H.
- HB is a useful middle value that is used for many purposes, not just for art.
- B is black and equates to soft graphite pencils ranging from B, 2B, to the softest 9B, which makes the darkest marks. Some manufacturers offer a wider range of soft pencils.
- F stands for fine, meaning that they can be sharpened to a fine point. These sit in the middle of the range from soft to hard.

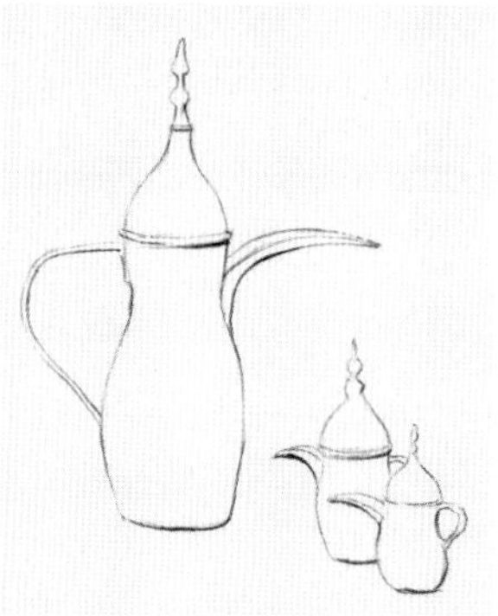

Graphite pencils create a variety of line weights: thin or interrupted lines denote areas where light hits the object, thick lines show shadow, and a variation of lines indicate form.

Charcoal

Charcoal is a manufactured product, made from burning wood at high temperatures in an oxygen-free situation. It can be used in various forms for drawing on a range of surfaces.

Charcoal pencils are wood-encased compressed charcoal, mixed with a binder that is usually gum or wax. Tinted charcoal pencils have muted colors. They are not easy to rub off and they will probably leave a mark, depending on the surface they are used on.

Charcoal sticks are either vine sticks, made from grape vines, or willow sticks, made from the twigs of willow trees. Both can be rubbed off and easily erased from the paper. Compressed charcoal sticks are harder, less prone to breakage, but can be difficult to erase.

Pencil Control and Hold

Drawing requires movement and pressure to make marks on a surface. A pencil can be held in different positions and at different angles to achieve a variety of effects.

When you write, the pencil is held firmly, usually near the sharpened end and only the hand and wrist move, maintaining controlled movements.

With drawing, there are a variety of holds but ultimately think of a soft hold on the pencil (held nearer the unsharpened end), with movement coming from the shoulder, allowing the arm to sweep gesturally across the surface. When more control is needed, reduce the movement and only move the arm from the elbow.

PENCIL PRESSURE

The amount of pressure you use will affect the marks you make. The harder you press, the darker the mark, but there is also a risk of damaging the paper if you press too hard. Graphite can become shiny when too many layers are laid down upon each other. To avoid these difficulties, use different grades of pencil to achieve your lighter and darker marks.

KEEP A STEADY HAND

It helps to use a mahl stick when drawing upright or to lean on something if working flatter. When drawing on location with no aids available, try keeping your upper arm close to your body for support, with movement coming from the elbow, not the shoulder.

Colored Pencils and Pastels

Colored pencils have centers filled with a mix of pigments, additives, and binding agents, encased in wood. They have differing proportions of ingredients resulting in some pencils being oil based with others wax based. Colored pencils have different lightfastness ratings, and some can fade very quickly. Make sure you buy the correct pencils for your use.

Pastel crayons are pure pigments mixed with little else and are best used on dedicated pastel paper. Soft pastels are easier to blend, giving a luxurious look and feel. Hard pastels work well for details and often produce less dust. A fixative spray can be used on finished pastel drawings, however, some artists feel this alters the look of the artwork.

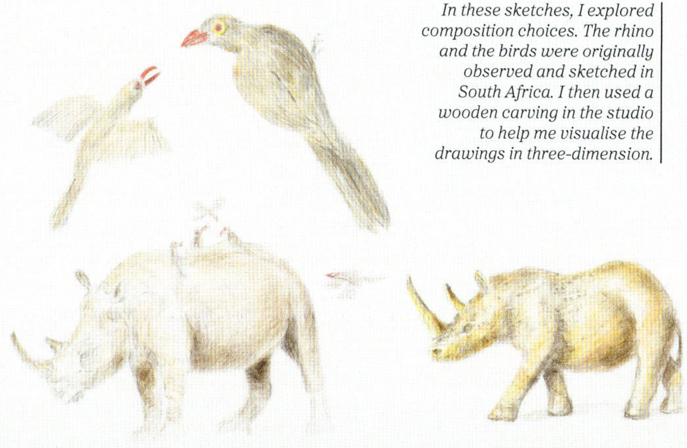

In these sketches, I explored composition choices. The rhino and the birds were originally observed and sketched in South Africa. I then used a wooden carving in the studio to help me visualise the drawings in three-dimension.

Pen and Ink

This is a drawing technique using a reservoir or dip pen with ink to create a variety of interesting marks.

Fountain and technical pens are types of reservoir pens, using refillable ink or ink cartridges. Ink usually flows from the nib with little pressure. Fountain pens are easy to carry for working on location and some fountain pens allow for interchangeable nibs.

Ballpoint pens and fiber-tipped pens come with ink pre-loaded. They don't create a variety of line weights and will eventually run dry. Waterproof ink versions of these pens are useful on location and can be used with watercolor washes.

Dip pens have handles with (usually) interchangeable nibs and do not have reservoirs of ink. They are dipped in ink and pressure is applied to the nib via the handle, which causes the nib to spread and release the ink. The nib has to be frequently dipped into an ink source during use, often after each stroke. There is a seemingly endless range of nibs available.

Drawing with a pre-loaded ink pen, such as a biro, fiber-tipped, or cartridge fountain pen makes working on location easy.

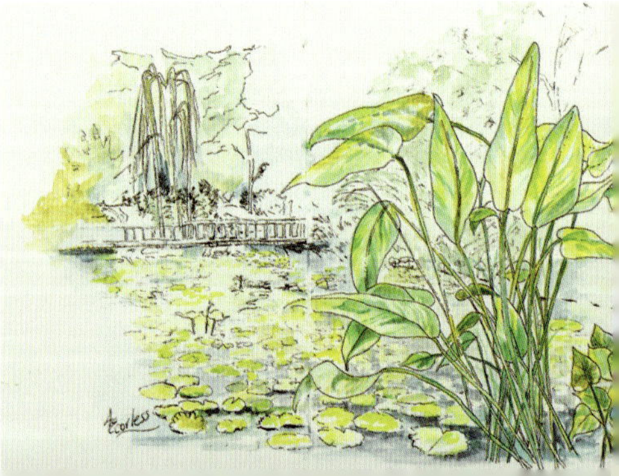

TYPES OF INK

Ink is either pigment-based or dye-based, and it is important to understand the qualities of both and to check their suitability for use with different pens and nibs. Always check the manufacturer's instructions before use.

Pigmented drawing inks are mostly waterproof and lightfast, as the pigment particles are suspended within a liquid. They will bleed less than dye-based inks.

Dye-based drawing inks contain pigments that are water soluble and fully dissolved in liquid. Colors are often vibrant and mix easily but can fade with time. Dye-based ink can usually be used with a broad selection of pens.

Additional Equipment

Here are some items that you may find useful on your drawing journey, but you certainly won't need all of them to get started:

- Drawing board
- Sharpener
- Masking tape
- Erasers (including kneaded eraser)
- Glassine paper (to protect drawing surfaces)
- Mahl stick (when working upright on an easel)
- Easel (floor standing and/or table top)
- Ruler
- Brushes for removing dust and blending
- Carbon and tracing paper
- Magnifying glass
- Plumb line with weighted end
- Gloves (to protect artwork from hand, cut the fingers off cotton gloves)
- Fixative spray (and NOT hairspray!)
- Apron

CHAPTER 2

Find Your Subject

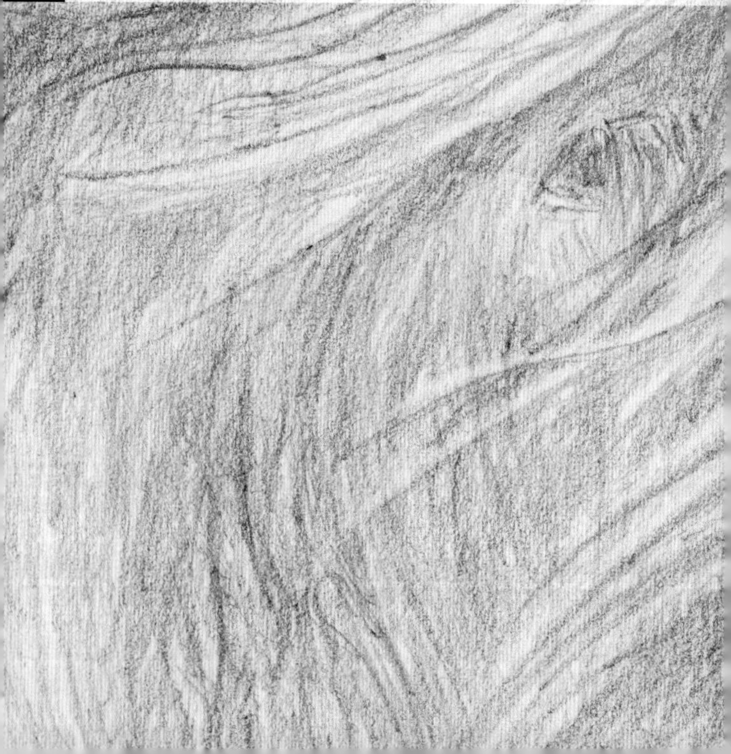

Choosing What To Draw

Finding a subject can seem daunting, until you remember that every artistic challenge you take on is really only just another small step in your creative journey. If you want to progress, you must persevere. Developing a good creative practice helps keep things on track. I have found that if I stick to my tried-and-trusted process, it enables me to be more creative and spontaneous with my artwork. So what do I mean by this?

A Creative Process

It helps to have a checklist. With experience, creative decision making becomes a quick and integral part of life as an artist. To help me decide what to draw, I ask myself the following four things.

What is the artwork for: if it's for my own creative development, then it's a good time to try new techniques and stretch my abilities without worrying about mistakes. It's all about enjoying the experience. If the artwork is a commission or a gallery piece, then it's usually best to stick with what I know I can do. Here, my drawing of the Singapore skyline during a Grand Prix race was for my own pleasure.

What materials do I have: I went prepared with a waterproof pen and a small sketchbook. This is enough for me to create some quick urban sketches.

What reference images do I need (if any): in this case, I was using my observational skills and drawing what I could see in front of me, as I was interested in the curved towers of the hotel and the observation deck. The rounded architecture, resembling a lotus flower, of the Art and Science Museum also caught my attention.

How much time is available: on this day, the weather dictated my plans with torrential rain during the day, resulting in my drawing a night scene.

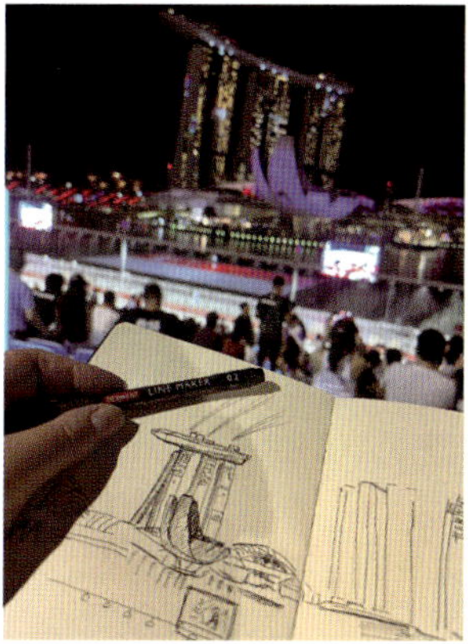

When urban sketching, I take pencils, a waterproof pen, eraser, and a sketchbook. That's all I need.

ENJOY THE PROCESS

By following the process, I was able to quickly and easily spot something to draw. Whatever route you take, don't worry about mistakes—it's all about enjoying the experience and spending time drawing. And it doesn't matter what you choose to draw it is the doing that counts!

Draw What You Know

Inspiration is all around us and it is easy to overlook the familiar, but start by drawing what you know. Everything has interesting shapes and textures: ornaments, jewelry, fruit. When you draw what you know, or what you can see and understand, you set yourself up for a good drawing session.

Pets are always a good choice to draw, and drawing a pet cat at rest gives you the opportunity to really study their shape and features. Drawing a long-haired cat can be more difficult as the body shape may be hidden. If this is the case, focus on the patterns of fur and facial features instead.

You don't have to draw only what you can see in real life. Any photo you take or object you own will work too. I have a carving of Asian elephants that is in a similar pose to an old photo of elephants I had taken when I lived in Kenya. Together, they gave me the information I needed to draw my African elephants.

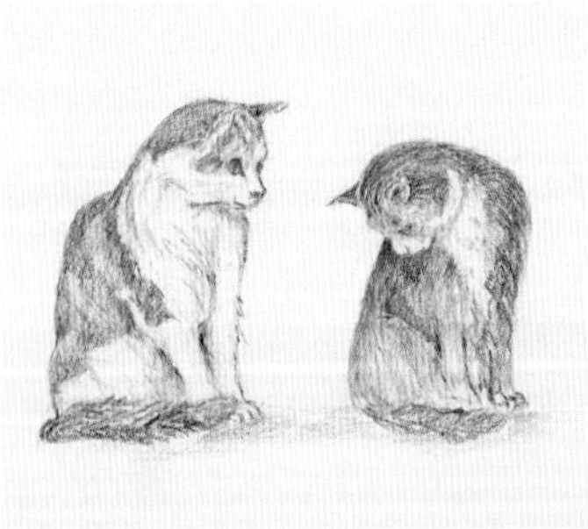

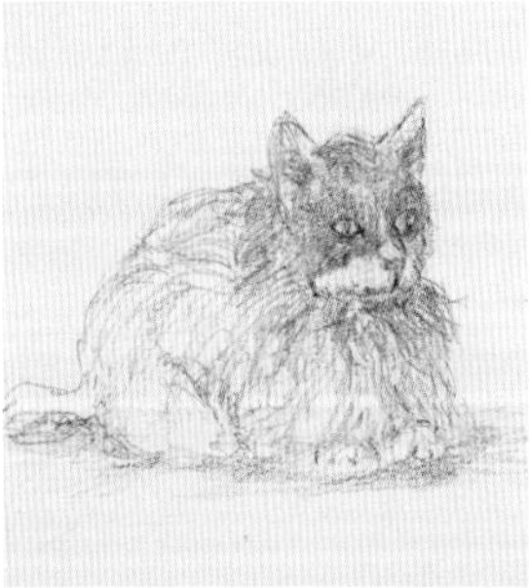

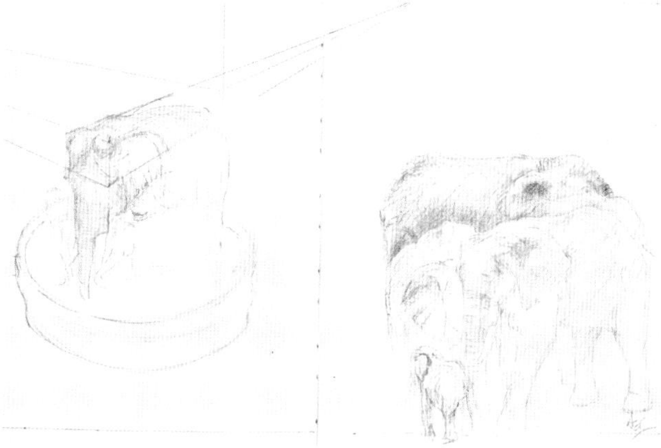

My treasured wooden carving of an Asian elephant family, from a trip to Thailand, is useful for giving me a three-dimensional view, much like the elephant group I spent hours watching at a waterhole in Kenya.

In this simple pencil drawing, the use of line weight gives the drawing weight and form. Thin interrupted lines along the top of the body are all that is needed to indicate shape. Thicker lines underneath the cat show weight and form.

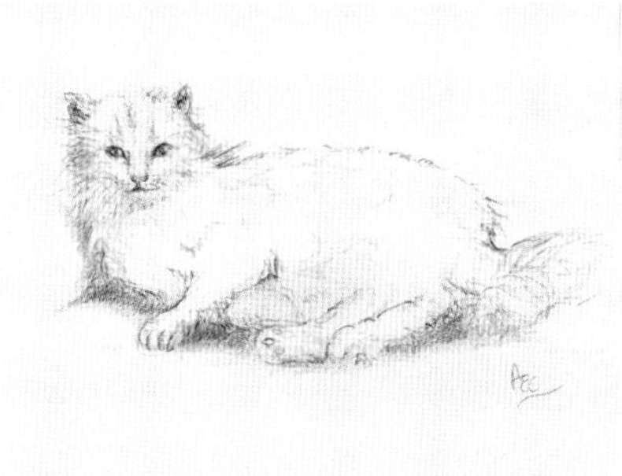

Sketching Outside

Drawing on location and urban sketching not only improves observational skills but also requires you to interpret what you see and decide how to draw it. What you draw does not have to be an exact copy of what you are viewing. You might be inspired to create an abstract, or only draw one small part of what you can see.

Finding your subject is often easier than you think, so try and understand what catches your interest and why. The more you look at the world around you with an artist's eye, the more you realize there are endless subjects to draw.

BROADEN YOUR CREATIVE HORIZONS

It takes a little bit of courage to draw in front of others, and drawing somewhere unfamiliar is a bit daunting, but it's important to push your creative horizons. Don't just sketch what you know or from photos. Try it!

I was a bit nervous to sit and observe the grandeur of the Summer Palace and Imperial Gardens in Beijing, China. It was unfamiliar to me but I was inspired to draw it. I started the drawing with a graphite pencil, mapping out the key features. Using a waterproof fineliner pen, I went over the pencil lines, correcting where necessary, and finally added a wash of watercolor. I probably spent just over an hour completing this sketchbook study on location.

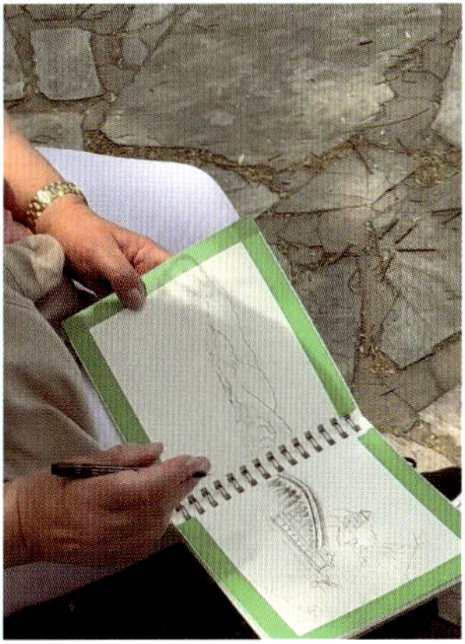

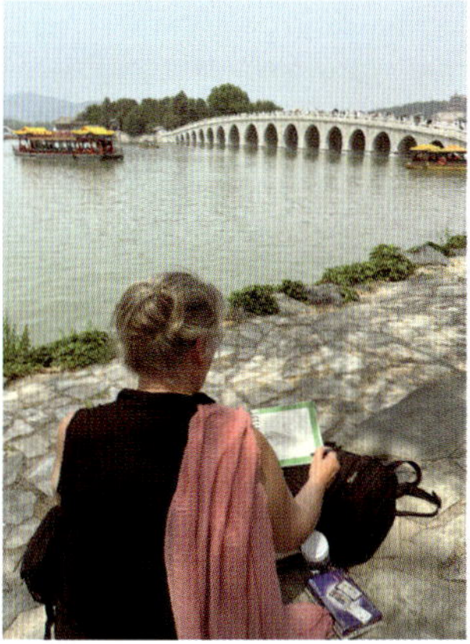

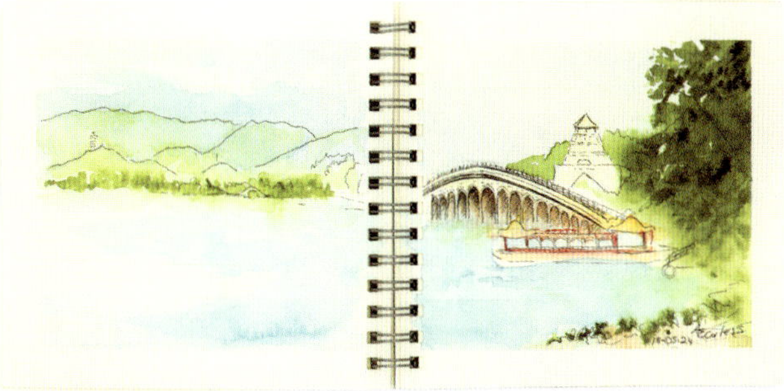

Applying masking tape to the pages of a sketchbook gives a nice white border when the work is complete and the tape removed.

Challenge Yourself

Finding your subject usually means looking for something to draw that captures your interest and looks achievable. However, if you find something that really captures your imagination but looks difficult, don't be put off. Have a go!

I had created a number of sketches while on a trip to Rome with my husband, and I was particularly drawn to the Trevi Fountain. That visit in itself was challenging, as the weather was hot, crowds of visitors disrupted my view, and time was limited. I still enjoyed the experience, however, and at the time, only thought of it as a way of building my drawing skills.

More recently, I re-discovered an old photograph of my mother and I sitting in front of the Trevi Fountain, taken many years ago. It evoked memories of happy times so it held a lot of meaning. I was inspired to draw it.

I was astounded when I realized that the sculpture of a Triton and hippocampus that we were in front of in the photo, was the same statue as I had drawn. It was a really challenging subject to take on but one I enjoyed. Never ignore something just because it looks too challenging.

And, don't worry if best laid plans go wrong! I often run out of space when sketching. Use masking tape if you want to add paper to extend the drawing. It might be messy, but it works and is fine for reference drawings.

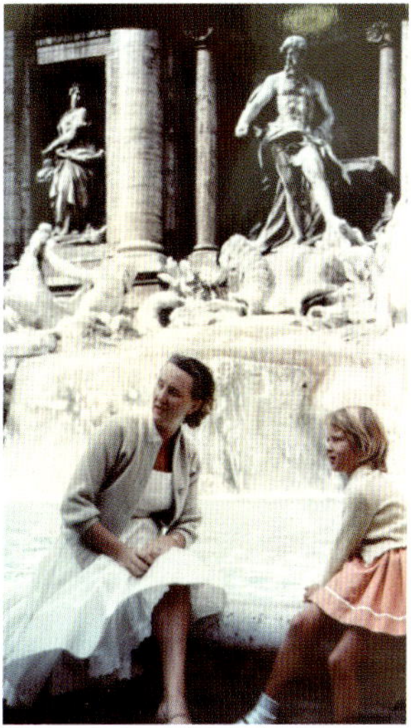

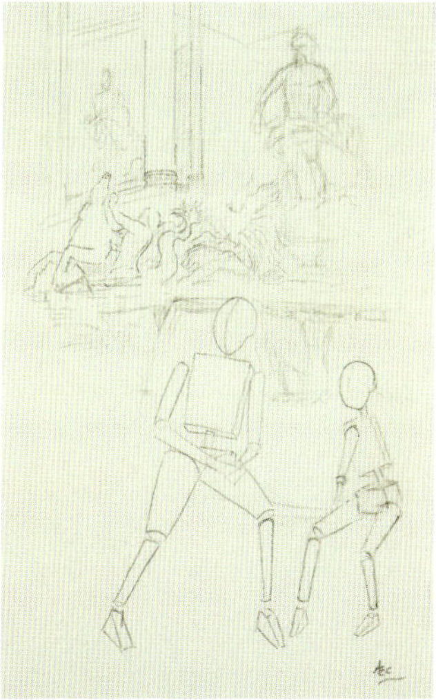

The dynamic movement of the sculptured horses and figures in the fountain, enhanced by the constant flow of water, is reinforced with shapes and curves. I found it easier to draw these complex dynamic shapes on location, using thin and thick lines to show depth and therefore form.

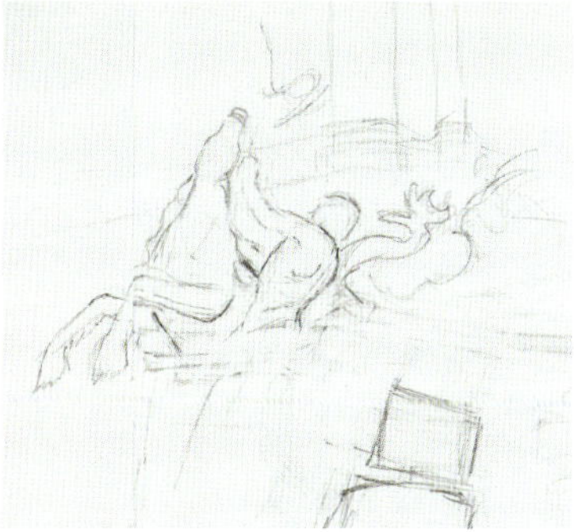

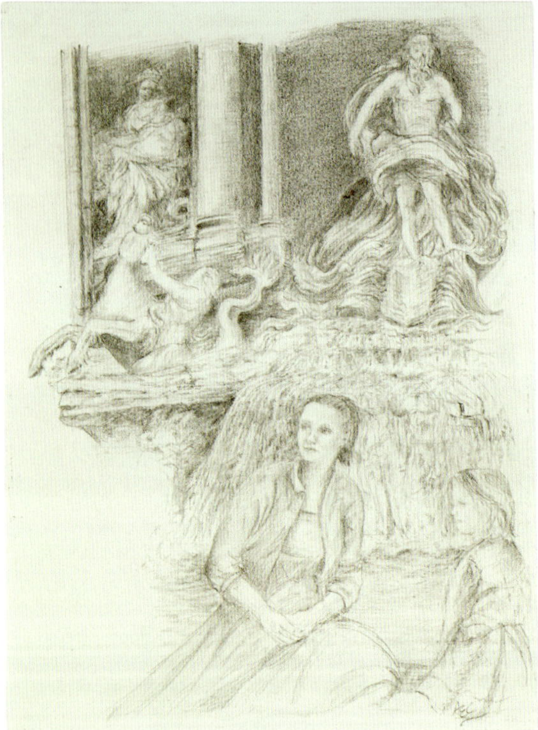

For a complex drawing such as this, it was necessary to make a preparatory drawing, with enough detail to check the placement of figures. I decided to cut off the bottom of the drawing at the level of the skirt, in the final artwork, to reflect the movement of clothing on the figure of Oceanus and the shell-shaped chariot.

TRY THIS: OBSERVE FORM AND MOVEMENT

When drawing any figure, be it from real life or a statue, you don't always need to draw every detail. Rather, it is better to indicate light and shade to give form to a drawing. You can practice how to give the impression of movement by looking in a full length mirror with a single light source and photographing or sketching your reflection. Even simple changes in body weight from one foot to the other, or movement of the limbs, will change what you see. Observe how the fall of clothing changes as your balance changes.

This sketch was done in Rome, and it didn't come out too badly, considering the challenges of drawing on the day, not least of which was a time issue!

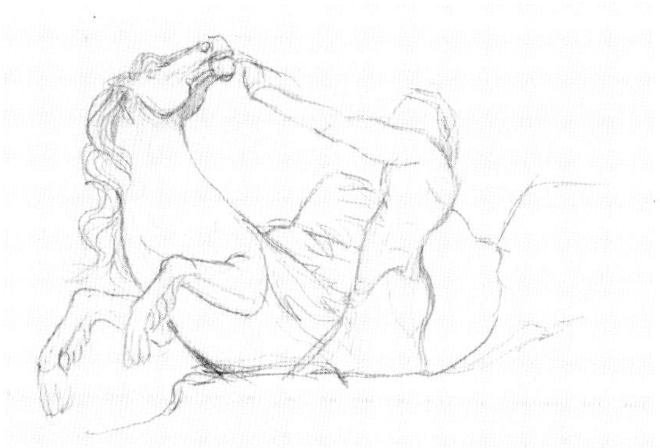

CHAPTER 3

Find Your Voice

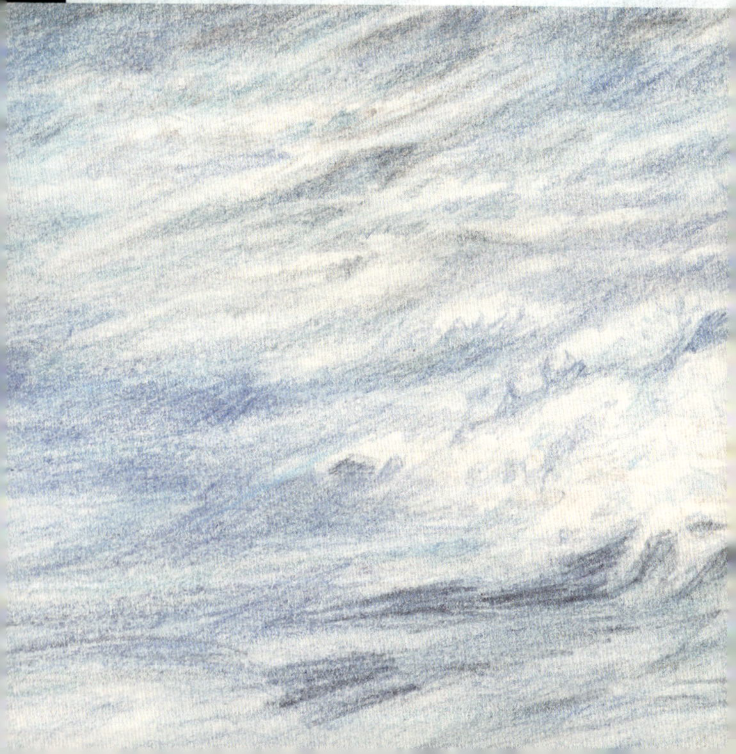

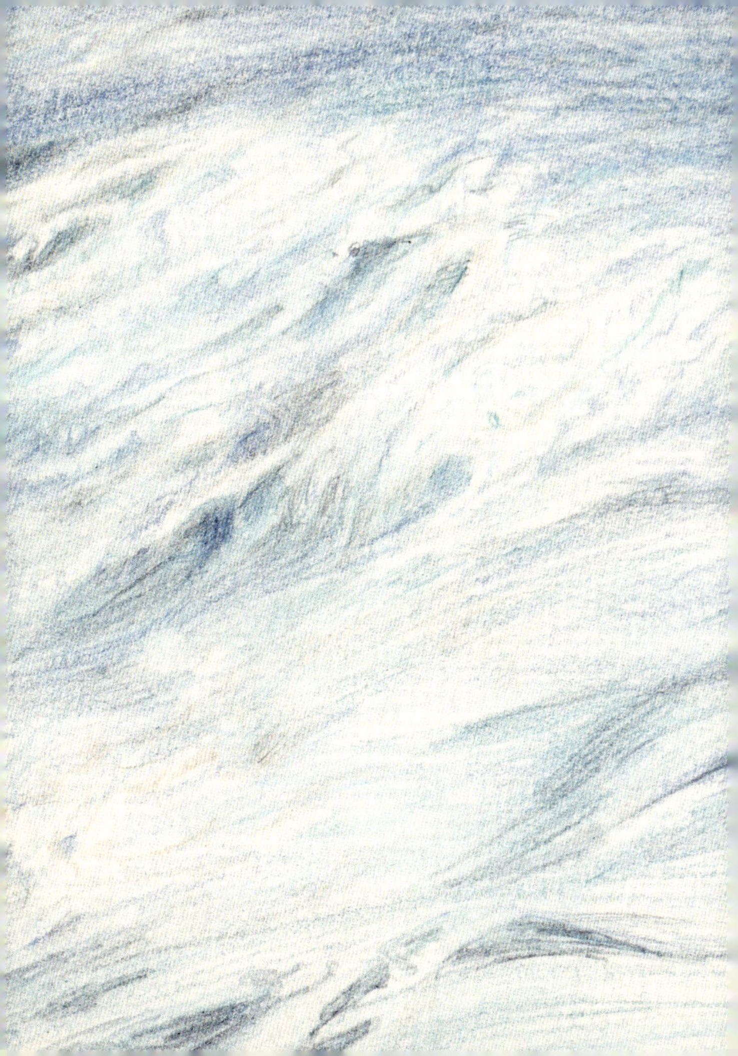

Discovering Your Style

Your creative voice is a uniquely individual and intuitive feeling about being an artist, how you approach creativity, and what you do with your art. For some, it is enough to spend time simply being creative, either alone or within a group. For others, a realization that art can be used to communicate ideas and views can take being creative into another realm, where art communicates messages and viewpoints. There is no right or wrong way to approach it but when you realize that the art you are creating is more than just a skill, that it can evoke emotion, then you start to recognize your creative voice.

Finding the Key

To find and recognize your own creative voice, you need an understanding of visual language, so it is wise to spend time learning your craft. Identifying your learning style is a good place to start. Are you someone who needs to work on course projects with the supervision of a teacher in a classroom situation or can you learn independently by doing your own research, watching online tutorials, and reading? There are many options to help you achieve your goals. I would suggest learning from an accredited skilled teacher, which should ensure that you are studying, and applying, what you really need to learn.

EXPECT THE UNEXPECTED

Always be prepared for unexpected moments of inspiration. I wanted to draw snowdrops on a crisp bright spring day at Lytham Hall, Lancashire, and so prepared some square templates to fit the flowers in. But an unexpected rainstorm appeared, sending me hurrying to find shelter. My immediate response was disappointment that my planned drawing was interrupted by the weather. The rain stopped and when I emerged it was as if I had been transported into a different world, changed by light and atmosphere. I decided to draw the trees instead, and of course they didn't fit into the pre-prepared squares! I encourage you to be flexible and not worry about other marks on the paper—go with what inspired you.

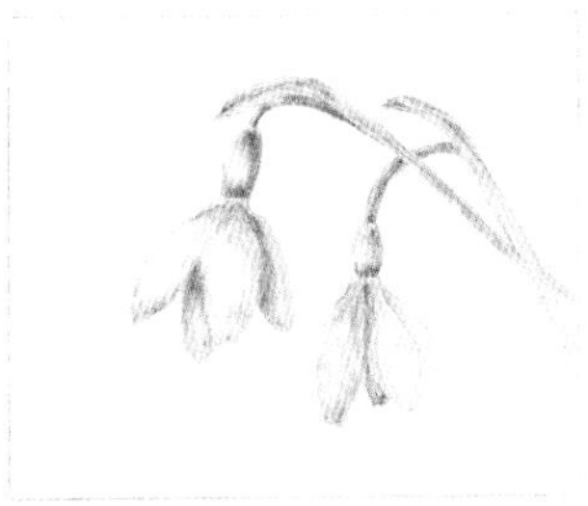

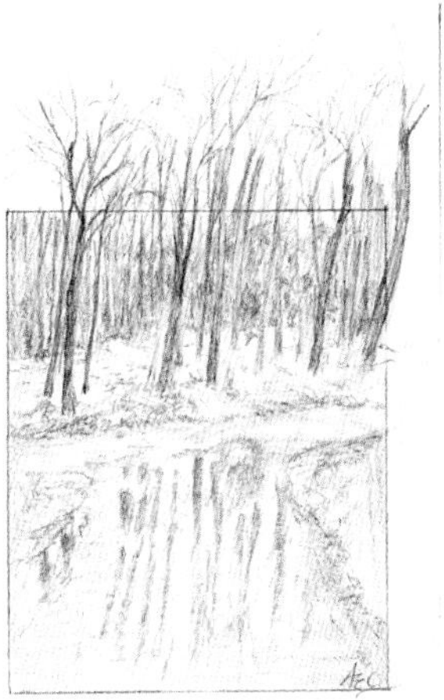

An unexpected drawing capturing the magic of light, atmosphere, and reflections after heavy rain.

Build Visual References

Building your own visual reference collection is an important aspect of your creative development. Setting aside time, when you can, to research, sketch, make up compositions, and write down your ideas, is actually one of the most useful things you can do. To the onlooker, it might look like a pointless activity but for the artist, it is these valuable moments spent thinking creatively that will enable you to find your own creative voice.

Take every opportunity to develop this collection of sketches and ideas. Every time you stop to observe and draw, you develop observation skills, you refine your drawing skills, you find the most effective way of drawing to suit the situation, and you develop visual memory. As your collection grows, you may find yourself wanting to spend more time on it, drawing more accurate sketches.

In this preparatory drawing of a clouded leopard, I tried to show how its anatomical adaptations allow it to climb trees in the forest.

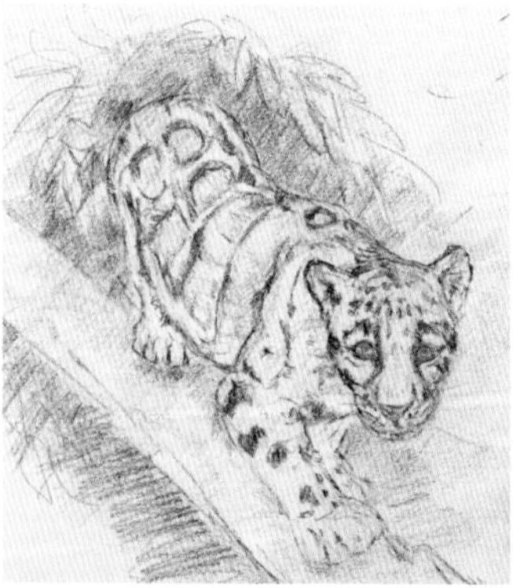

A NOTE ON PHOTOGRAPHS

Photographs can be suitable to work from as reference but remember that some lens distortion can occur. For that reason, it is helpful to sketch and gather different views of a subject, preferably in good lighting conditions, so that you can identify a good value range of lights and darks.

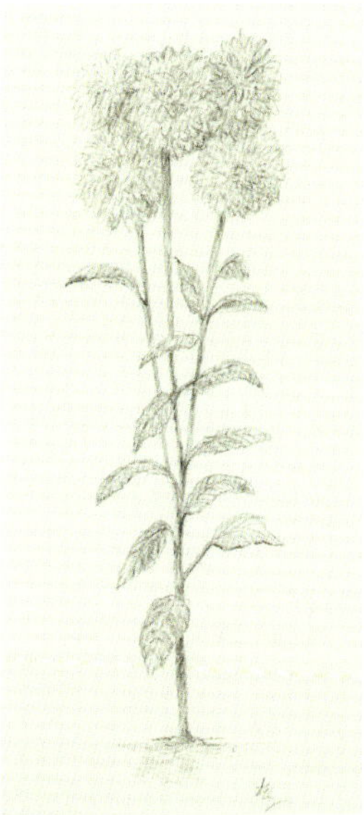

For my visual reference collection, it was important for me to draw a full dahlia flower, but I also focused in on the shapes of the petals. It might inspire another artwork one day!

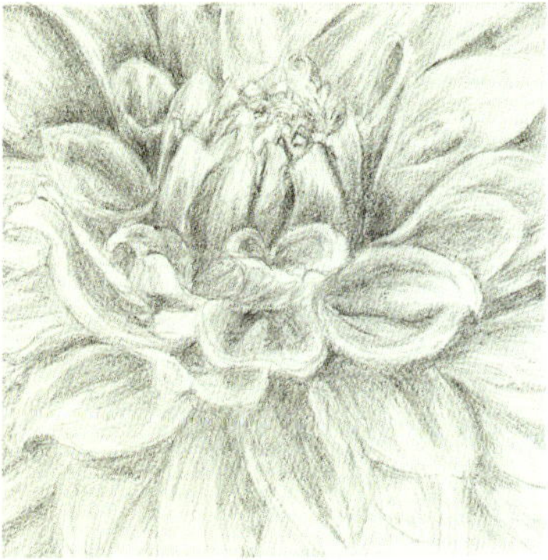

Don't restrict yourself to only using photos as references. Just as trying to work out compositions on a very small piece of paper can cause you to unknowingly restrict creative marks, so using photographs alone can have an unintended effect. It may seem easier to recreate a photo exactly, but are you missing out on design possibilities if you do?

However, in some cases, it is important to use a camera, such as to avoid disturbing wildlife by getting too close. These three gull chicks were protected by a huge mother gull, so to ensure I kept my distance, and not be attacked, I used a camera to take reference photos and also did some quick sketches to be finished back in the studio.

With mottled feathers, the chicks were camouflaged by reeds and the constantly moving, reflected lights and shadows of the water. When they approached the rock, their shapes became easier to see, as their fluffy feathers starkly contrasted with the rock.

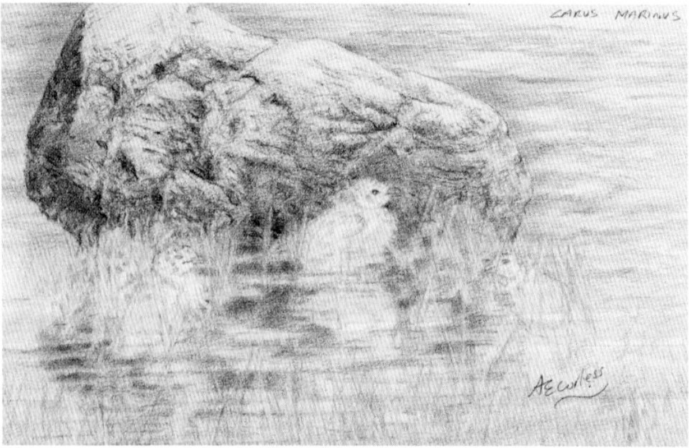

This sketch of the adult gull was also done on location and finished back in the studio, checking identifying features against reference information.

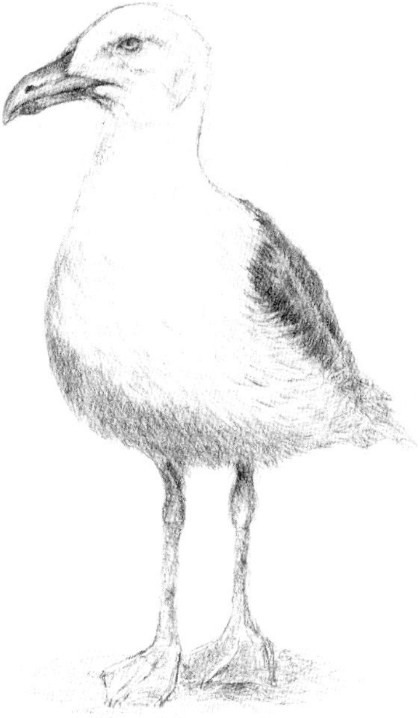

Develop Observational Skills

Sometimes a scene can captivate for moments only, so be on the lookout for something that has creative interest and get drawing. You will need to *always carry a sketchbook!*

Here, a scenic sunset had enough differences in shapes and values to be visually interesting but then I saw a barn owl perched on an aerial.

I have other reference images and memories of seeing barn owls, so my design decision was to leave a closeup of the owl to another day. My creative instinct was to show the simple shapes of urban objects with the beautiful owl—a happy addition that serves to reinforce that the natural world is just outside our door. It shows you don't have to draw detail if you can't see it, as the overall image is appealing and worthy of being sketched.

Hatching and cross hatching define each area in this preparatory drawing. The negative space of the sky makes the owl more prominent. If I had included more of the buildings, the owl might not be so easily noticed.

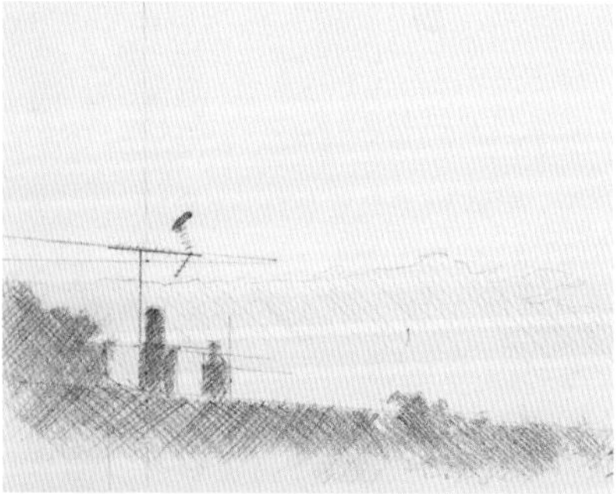

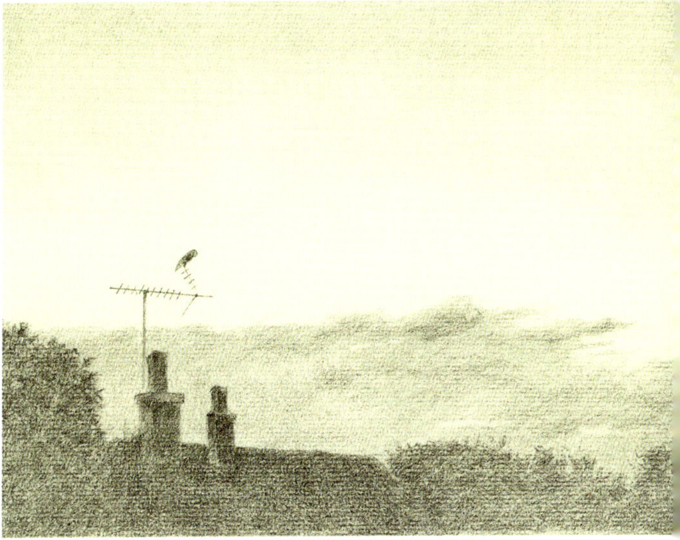

The final artwork is rendered more heavily using HB, B, and 3B graphite pencils on a slightly textured paper (suitable for charcoal), which adds interest. Hatching, cross hatching (often turning the paper whilst drawing), and irregular mark making fill in the tooth of the paper. The outline shape of the owl is better defined against a brighter band of sky.

Imagination

Use your imagination in your artwork. When deciding on your next project, it may seem easier to look for a reference to draw from, but why not turn it around: think of an idea first, and then source your own reference images?

When working this way, your artwork becomes a form of storytelling, so it helps to write down your ideas for future reference. Once you are no longer limited by only trying to recreate what you see, you may find a new confidence as you experience the thrill of coming up with your own creative ideas. Using your imagination when drawing can make it more fun.

Even though these drawings of the windmill look different, the shape of the building is the same, other than the sails being at different angles. Pen and ink is ideal for such a subject. The addition of a watercolor wash seen here, enhances the beauty of the windmill, the sun bouncing off its rounded walls.

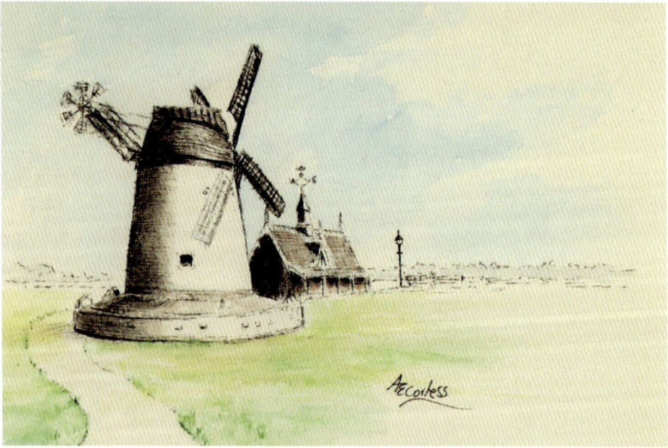

My aim with this artwork was to come up with an imaginative way of drawing the windmill on Lytham Green. I used sketches to try a few ideas for a final artwork and each ended up telling a different story. The first emphasizes billowing coastal clouds, with winds that would have turned the sails. The second shows the situation of the windmill next to an estuary in a coastal town.

In these two pen and ink preparatory drawings, I explored options for a composition. In the first study, a stormy sky contrasts strongly with the windmill. In the second study, the estuary is featured with the windmill in the distance. It would be impossible to draw from this position, so imagination is needed. I am bound to return to this subject many times, so each artwork of it is part of my own creative development.

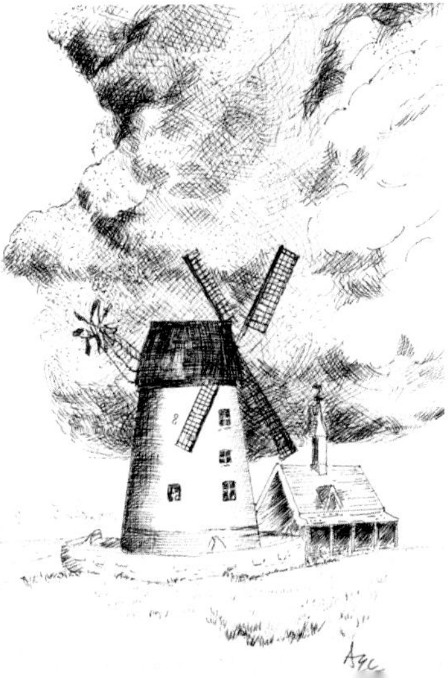

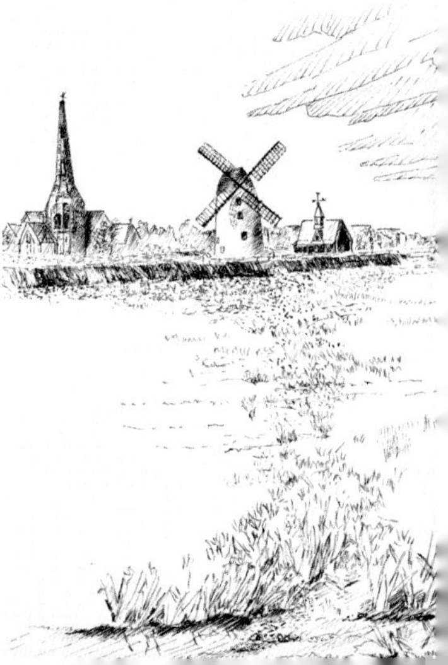

TRY THIS: WRITE A MISSION STATEMENT

Developing a creative practice is just one part of learning how to be creative. It is also important to think about what you want to say as an artist, to develop your creative voice. Acknowledge that you are on a creative journey and start talking about your own art and what interests you about other artists.

Write down (perhaps in a sketchbook) where you think you are now, in terms of how much time you dedicate to your art, what skills you have learned, and if you have reached out to meet other artists or groups. Then write down what your next steps are and what you want to achieve on your creative journey. This is your first mission statement!

The Loen Skylift near Olden, Norway is one of the world's steepest cable cars but what a view! I nearly lost my hat and the sketchbook while drawing this in extremely windy conditions.

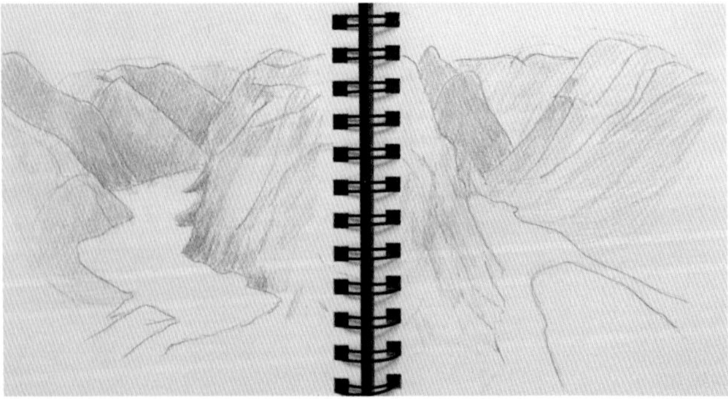

Artist Insight

The Golden Age of the High Renaissance in Italy was from the late 15th to the early 16th century. Studying the works of Leonardo da Vinci (1452–1519), Michelangelo (1475–1564), and Raphael (1483–1520) reveals the detailed preparatory drawings made before painting.

The Dutch Golden Age in the 17th century saw Flemish painters Peter Paul Rubens (1577–1640) and Rembrandt van Rijn (1606–1669) overseeing workshops teaching essential art skills including drawing the human figure. Painting subjects had moved away from religious symbolism of the past to representing the natural world and everyday life. Behind every masterpiece created by Rembrandt and Rubens were collections of preparatory studies in pencil, chalk, and watercolor.

CHAPTER 4

Practical Techniques

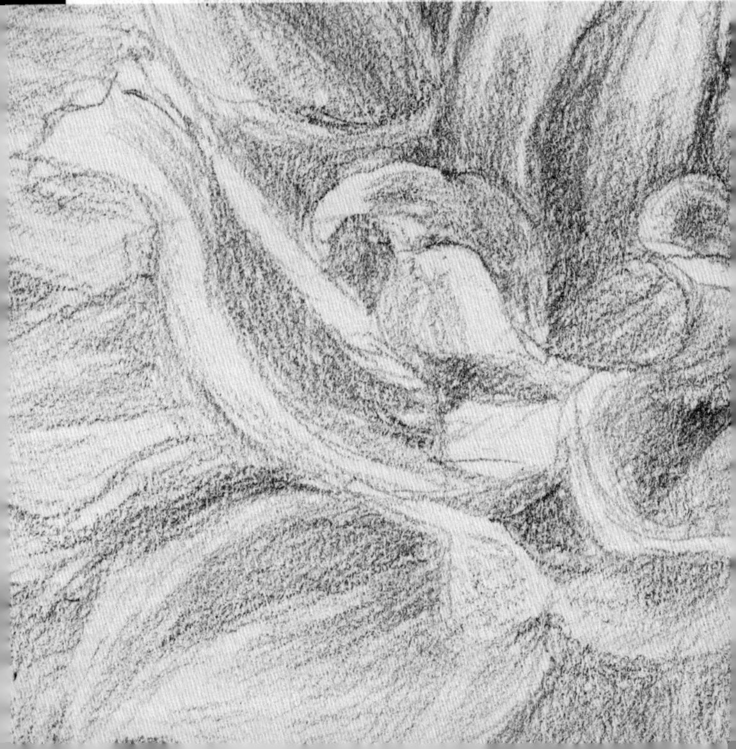

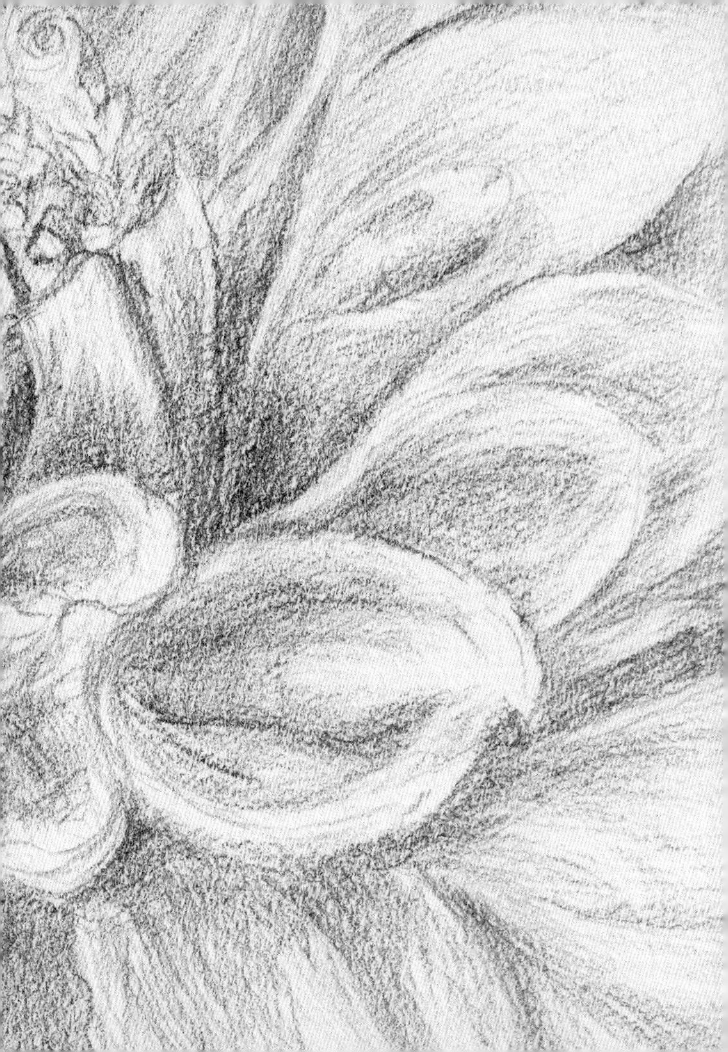

Learning to Use Your Tools

Learning how to draw involves developing observational skills and creative decision making based on an understanding of art materials and techniques, and then allowing time for practice. With this mix of information and skills, a creative process will evolve, a way of working that helps you achieve results and creates an environment within which to hone skills. In this chapter, we will discuss artwork created with line only, before moving on to tonal artwork, and finally, we will introduce texture.

Getting Started

It's wonderful to feel the creative urge and to want to start drawing immediately. However, let's take a moment to look at some principles of art.

Lines are a continuous mark of varying length and weight, used to draw shapes and dimensions. Lines can be decorative or abstract.

Shapes are two-dimensional enclosed areas such as squares and circles.

Texture is the surface quality of the artwork.

Form is the volume of an object, giving the impression of depth. If form is not shown in a drawing, it will appear flat.

Color is made up of hue (the color), value, and saturation (or chroma).

Value is the lightness and darkness of color and tone.

Line Artwork

Line artwork is useful to quickly capture outlines and shapes. The quality of the line created is called the line weight. Often a thinner, less dark line suggests that light is falling on a subject. An interrupted line can have the same effect. A darker, thicker line usually suggests an area in shadow. Gestural lines tend to be more organic and give an indication of attitude and movement: think of a cat about to pounce and a curved imaginary line along its length from nose to tail. It might not be possible to capture detail in such situations, but a gestural line can capture the intention and movement.

A biro is all I could find when we approached Iceland, so I tried to capture the rugged beauty of the coastline. Strong lines and hatching gives the drawing depth.

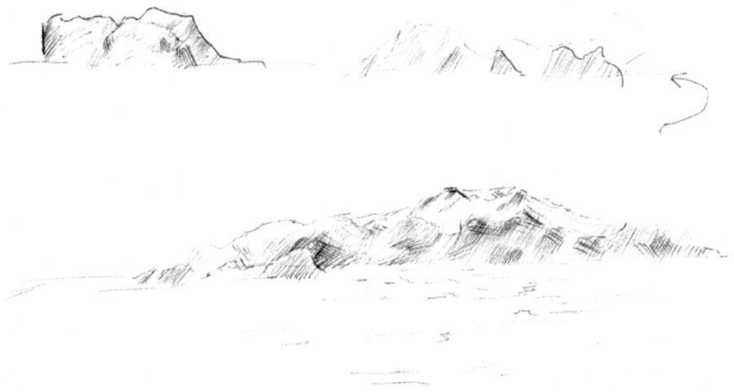

FROM PENCIL TO PEN

Working with line is my preferred way to record shapes, especially when there is limited time to capture tonal values. On a cruise off the coast of Newfoundland and Labrador, there was no time to do nice tonal drawings or even a watercolor painting as the conditions on deck were cold and windy! After sketching the icebergs in pencil from life, I quickly drew copies with a waterproof pen, back in the warmth of the cabin, to clearly define shapes and planes.

Line drawings capture shapes quickly. This sketch was later copied and drawn using a pen.

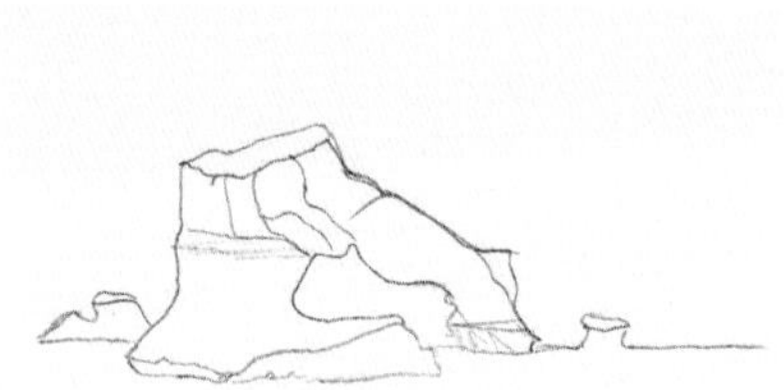

Line and tone of the iceberg from a different angle to the one above. This is also from a pencil drawing but having just seen the iceberg, I was able to remember the effects of the light and shade.

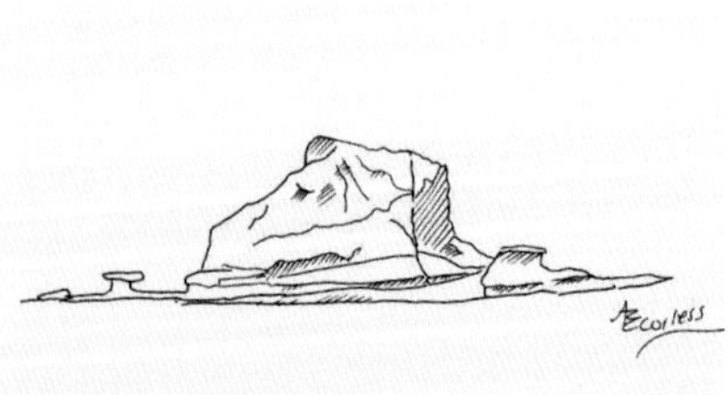

Tonal Drawing

This is the use of shading to create form. By hatching and cross hatching, or even stippling on a drawing, it is possible to describe form (making the object appear three-dimensional). An area onto which the light falls will appear lighter than an area in shadow. When you squint at an object, you are reducing the detail you can see, which makes it easier to identify the differing areas of light and dark. Learning to interpret value is key, and using a value scale will help you identify them (see Chapter 6 for more on value).

A tonal drawing done from a small moving boat shows how few marks are needed to describe a scene.

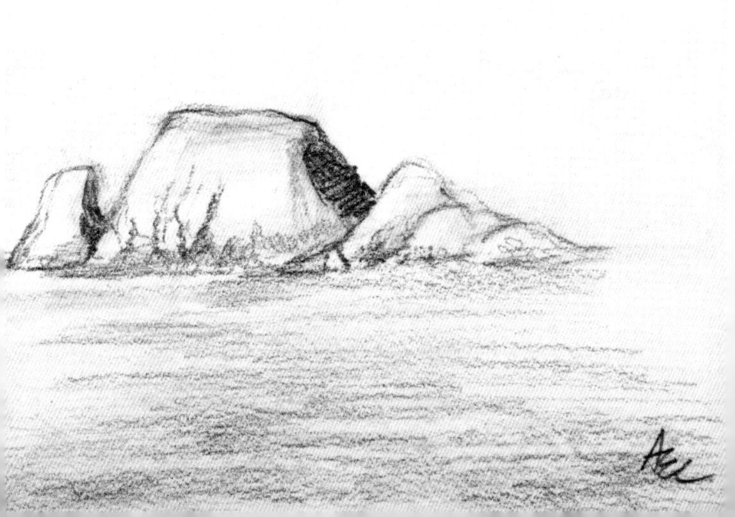

In beautiful Andalsnes, Norway, it was the dramatic changing light of an approaching storm in the distance, that caught my attention, contrasting with the calm water in the fjord in the foreground. The sketch below was immediate and raw, as if I was making visual notes of elements to be included in a final artwork.

Charcoal is ideal for creating subtle changes in value, so I used it for the final drawing. Having drawn simple shapes, I decided where the light, mid, and dark values should be and built the drawing gradually, reassessing values as it progressed.

This dramatic sky demonstrates a range of values from light to dark with shades in between. It's hard to describe but easy to see!

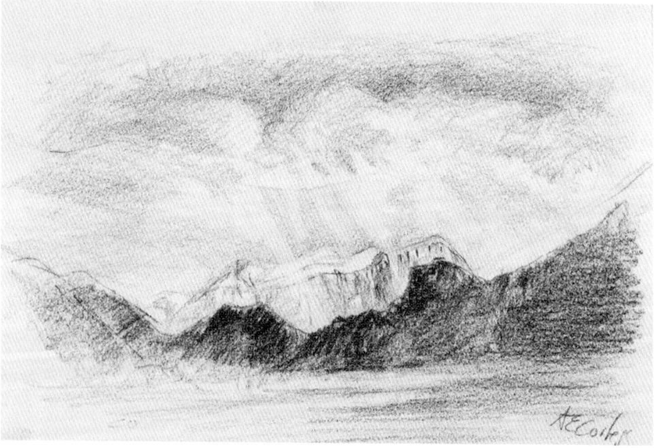

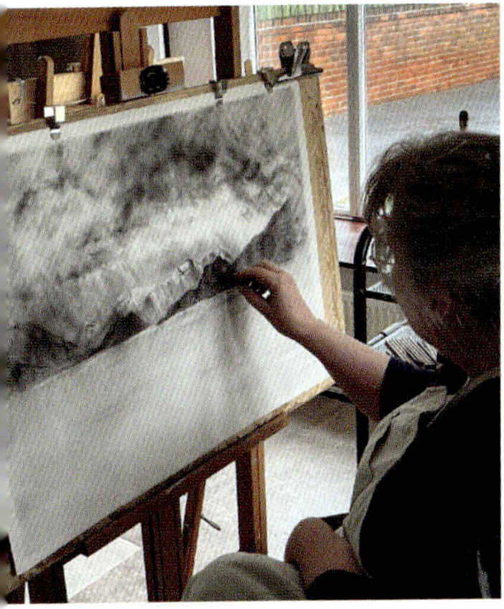

Working at an easel allows you to clearly see and assess the composition and perspective. View artwork from a distance and look back at it in from a mirror (to reflect the image).

The final artwork includes a number of elements: the sky (and how much it takes up in the composition), mountains of the fjord, the sea, and the causal factor–the weather. The focus is on light and shadow, and contrast.

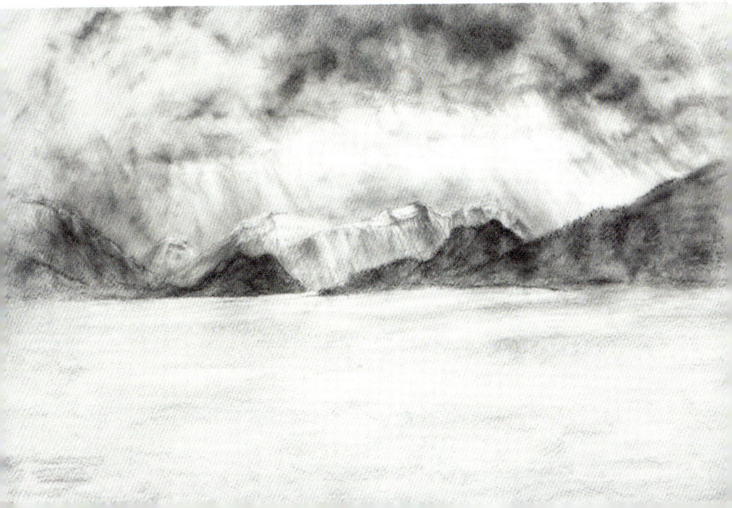

Understanding Form

Learning how to draw form involves understanding that light is reflected from objects onto which it falls, causing some areas to be in light and some to be in shadow.

Being able to see value, the range of lights and darks on a subject, comes with practice. Drawing this pelican, with entirely opposite feather colors to the ibis, was a good exercise in how light falling on an object allows us to see form. Note how the edges of the bird in areas such as the beak are hard ("found" edges are clear to see) whereas parts of the body seem to disappear into the background with soft (indistinct "lost") edges. There is a gradual rounding of the body away from the light source. There are highlights, mid-tones with half tones, and shadow areas, as well as cast shadows. The dark background gives a suggestion of the pelican's environment.

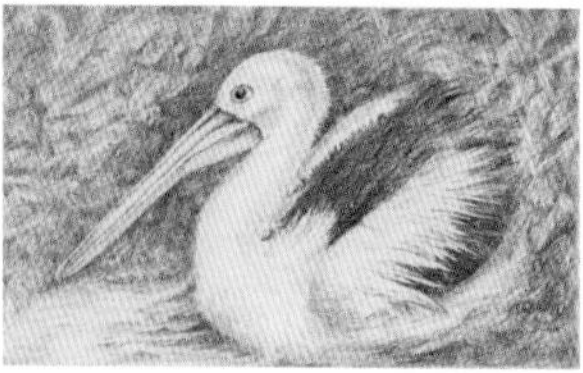

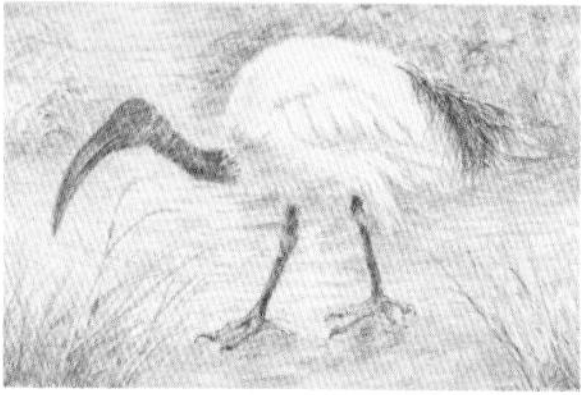

The pelican has a white head and the dark background reveals the shape, so you almost don't need to draw an outline of the bird's head. Conversely, the ibis has a dark head and so needs to be drawn and rendered. The background has a light value to add contrast.

TRY THIS: OBSERVE LIGHT AND SHADOW

1

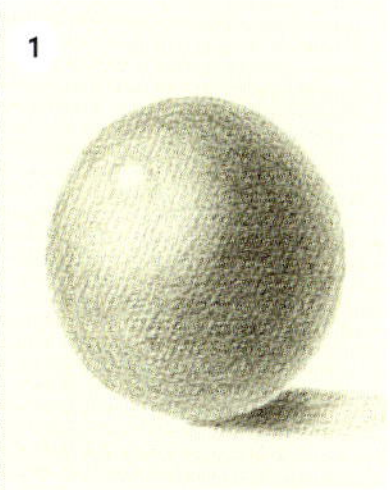

2

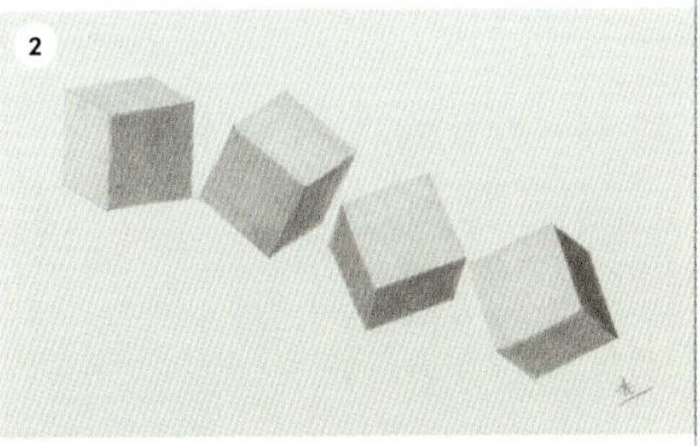

1. On a sphere, with a single light source, there are subtle changes of light, from a highlight to mid-tones (subtle halftones) to shadow areas, with a cast shadow (from the sphere) falling on the surface below.

2. On a cube, with a single light source, there are transitions, often sharp, from light to dark at an edge. The value of each side changes depending on the amount of light reaching it. No cast shadows are seen in this drawing as the cubes tumble.

Texture and Details

Adding texture to artwork is a means of visually describing the look and feel of a subject, and can be added with a variety of marks. Hatching and cross hatching can add uniformity whereas scribbled lines and irregular stippling suggests unevenness and even serve as a warning to take care when touching.

As a wildlife artist, I try to show features of the animals I draw. The African elephant has thick, gray wrinkled skin but in most of my artwork of the elephants, seen in Kenya, they appear red due to the color of the soil they throw over themselves as a sunscreen and for insect protection. Elephant ears are thinner with blood vessels near the surface of the skin to cool the elephant, which you can see in this drawing.

Hatching and cross hatching are effective ways of showing both form and texture. Deeper shadows are achieved by increasing the line weight and changing the direction of the lines, so they criss-cross over each other.

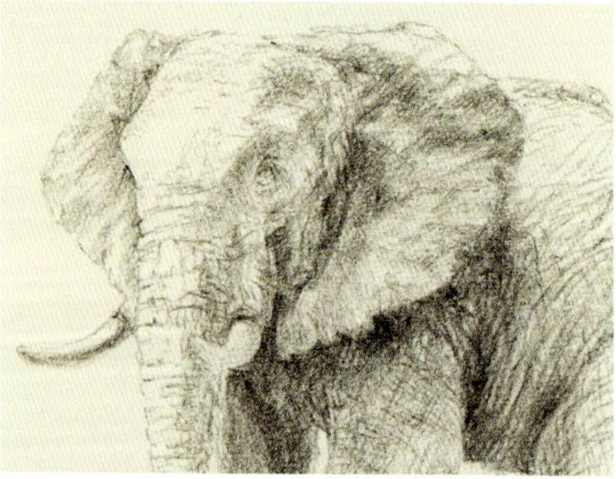

Don't try and force texture. When I start making marks on the paper, even on smooth paper, allowing the layers to build over each other usually results in some sort of pattern appearing. Sometimes, even a surprising texture reveals itself. I know the texture will appear, I just need to be patient to let it build. If I make a mistake, I leave it and move on. With textured work, misplaced marks may not be of any consequence in the end.

ADD CONTRASTING ELEMENTS

Introduce contrast within each drawing to add interest, and you can use the technique of lost and found edges (see Understanding Form). When I suggest texture in a drawing, I often use expressive and abstract marks in varying values so that not everything is clear. It is a means of introducing mood, atmosphere, or tension and I often balance this in a composition against a highly detailed focal point.

Even on sketchbook paper, it is possible to make textural marks. Here we have a rock, water with reflections, smooth reeds, and fluffy chicks, all created with a graphite pencil!

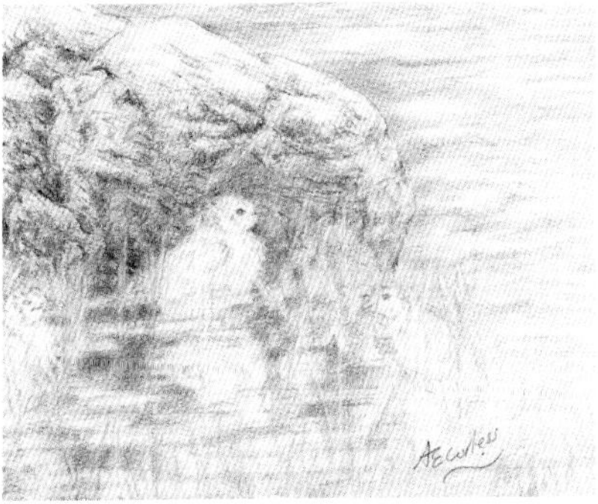

PENCIL CRAFT

Keep your pencil sharpened to draw fine or accurate lines. As the lead wears down, rotate the pencil every now and then for more even wear. When laying down value, use a more rounded end. A sharp tip might catch on the paper leaving a dark mark that is hard to remove or disguise.

As your drawing skills and confidence improves so "feel" develops. You begin to work out how hard to press down on the paper with a pencil and how developing a relaxed drawing hand and body position will allow you to make subtle changes in pencil pressure. It becomes a physical experience where you feel the sensations of drawing, hear the sound of pencil on paper, and notice the smell of art materials.

Inspired by different experiences of seeing elephants, I choose techniques to reinforce the impressions made. An elephant drinking in the midday sun with strong contrasting light is ideal for pen and ink.

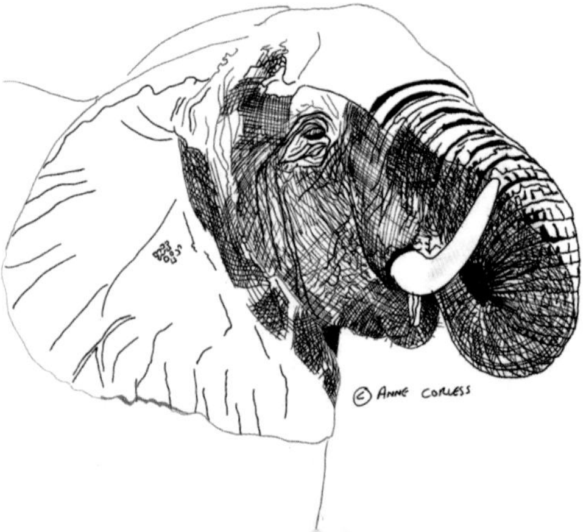

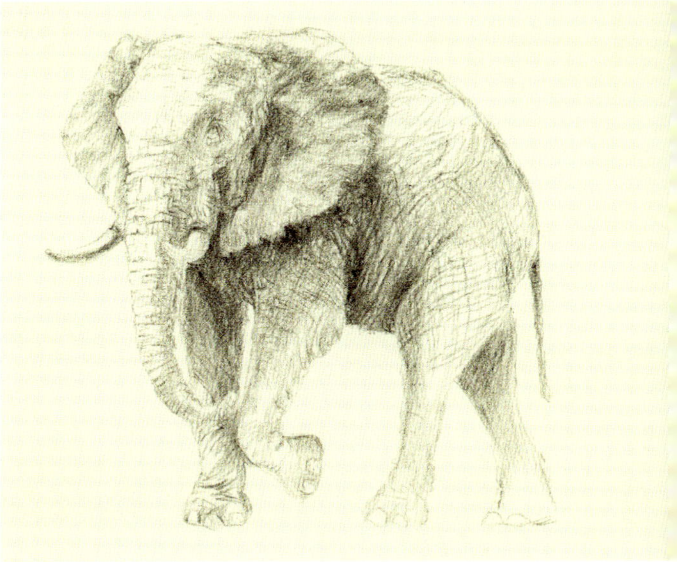

Even on a plain background, you can add as little or as much detail as you want, though not all areas of a drawing require detail.

Practicing art techniques, using different techniques, keeping all your sketches and studies, and working to advance your skills means that when inspiration and opportunity arise to be creative, you will have choices, and know which to choose to reinforce your story.

CHAPTER 5

Understanding Composition

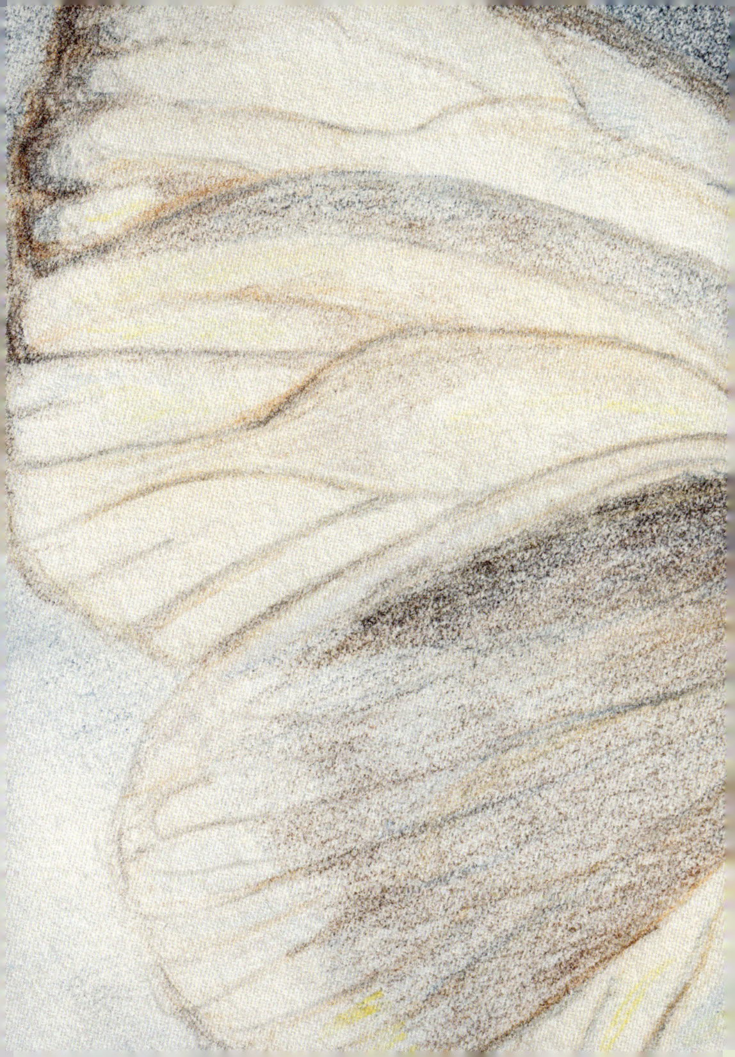

Arranging Your Artwork

Composing your artwork simply means deciding what to include and where to place elements on your paper. A simple composition, such as a drawing of a pet, may only include one element but it still requires decision making; whether to draw only the pet's head to capture detail and expression or whether to include the full body, requiring less detail. More complex compositions, involving more than one element, bring other considerations into play such as spatial awareness, comparative sizes, proportion, and perspective.

Designing Your Composition

Decide on your subject, sketch out ideas in thumbnails, and write down any other ideas. Think about what the focal point is and if other elements need to be given the same emphasis. Try using the Rule of Thirds, where the paper is divided into three each way and important elements are placed on intersecting lines. The Golden Ratio is also favored by some.

Ask yourself if you need to include everything you see, for instance, do you need to draw everything in a landscape? Be creative and make your own design decisions. Why not detract from a problem area by placing something in front of it? This is often a work around to solve a compositional problem. Once you use this device, you will begin to notice how other artists do the same. Me included!

The planning and composition stage can be a fun part of the process and you may be surprised at how many composition options you come up with. Even when you've decided on a composition, be sure to keep all options you drew, as they may serve as an inspiration for future work.

This sketch of the Singapore skyline was drawn quickly from the boat I was standing on, which you can see in the foreground.

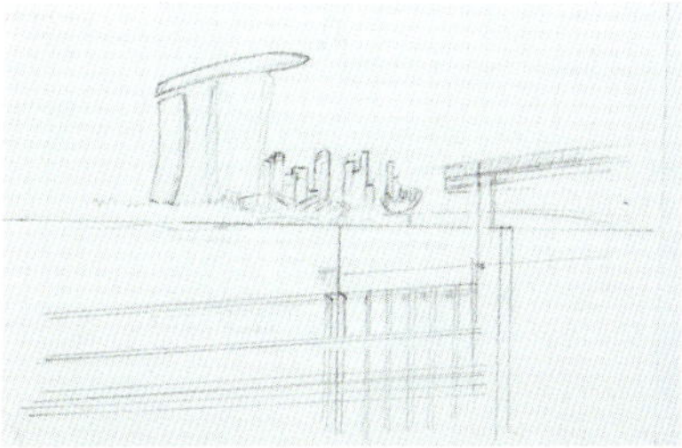

Back in the studio, I set about drawing the shapes of the buildings, trying to keep it simple. Working through different thumbnail drawings, I came up with a simple composition.

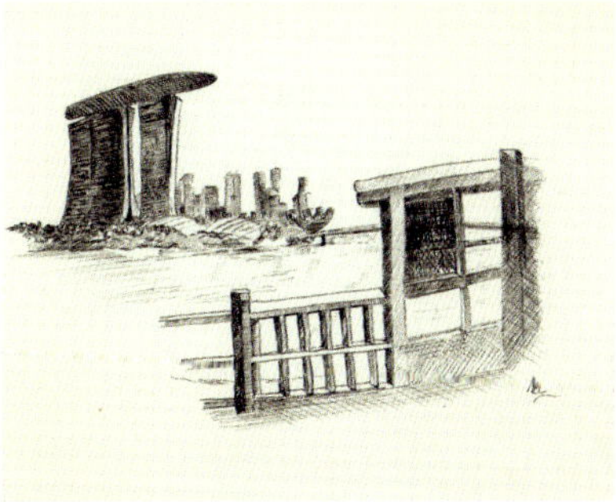

Understanding Visual Language

To better grasp composition, you need to develop an understanding of spatial awareness, positive and negative spaces, and different types of perspective.

The picture plane is your drawing surface, a view into a two-dimensional world you are creating that involves drawing three-dimensional objects within that world. Spatial awareness is the ability to manipulate all the elements in your drawing, using art techniques such as perspective. Perspective makes sense of objects within a flat two-dimensional artwork.

LINEAR PERSPECTIVE

Linear perspective comprises parallel lines, a vanishing point, and a horizon line. Think of railway tracks: they are parallel but they appear to converge on the horizon, which is the effect of linear perspective. Linear perspective can be one-, two-, or three-point perspective. My illustration is an example of one-point perspective, meaning that the lines on the jetty receding into the distance would, eventually, converge to one point.

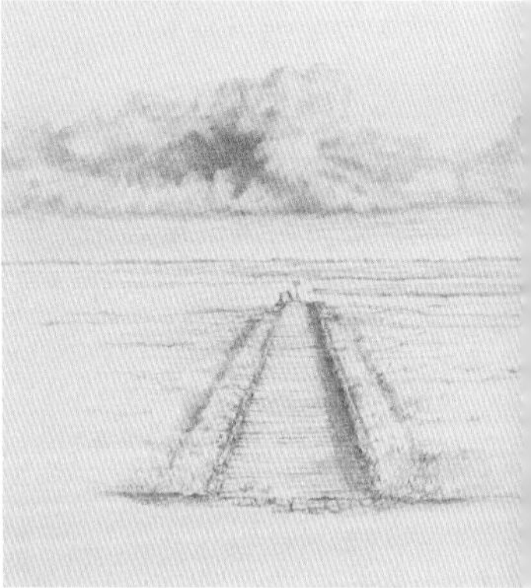

This preliminary drawing of Lytham Jetty shows how the parallel lines of the jetty converge (and would meet at the vanishing point) on the horizon. People standing at the end of the jetty look smaller than they would at the start of the jetty, in the foreground.

ATMOSPHERIC PERSPECTIVE

Aerial or atmospheric perspective is the effect of the atmosphere, full of gases, dust, and moisture on light waves. Blue light waves are shorter, scatter easily, and are therefore more readily seen. An example of this can be seen in landscape drawings with distant views. Objects in the foreground are sharper with a range of colors, whereas distant objects tend to have a blue tint with less definition.

POSITIVE AND NEGATIVE SPACE

When the sun sets and light fades, details disappear. Objects become shapes. Shadows elongate. In my composition below, the birds are a dominant dark color (positive shapes) and there is space around them (negative shapes) for the light on the shoreline to be seen. My aim was to show the abstract design of the birds amidst the last remaining remnants of daylight.

There is some overlapping of the birds to show depth and to capture movement. Keeping perspective in mind, I have ensured the birds nearer to me are larger than those in the distance.

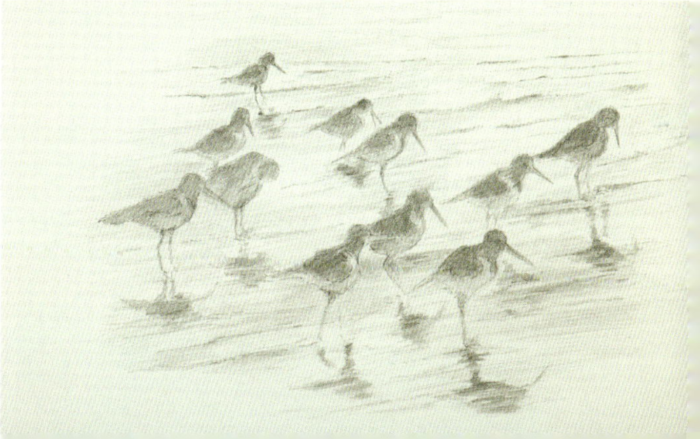

Mixing References

To make a composition you need different elements, and these can come from different places. In this project, I used a previously painted seascape (watercolor) and combined it with a Norther Fulmar skimming over the sea. I had studied and drawn the bird from life, angled in flight, and it gave me the visual references to work out a composition, being mindful of perspective and lighting.

Drawing a moving bird is easier to manage if you think of your visual references as a guide and then draw the shapes you want, where you want! Here, the placement of the bird was deliberate. These birds fly low and to show just how low, I placed it in a trough between two large waves.

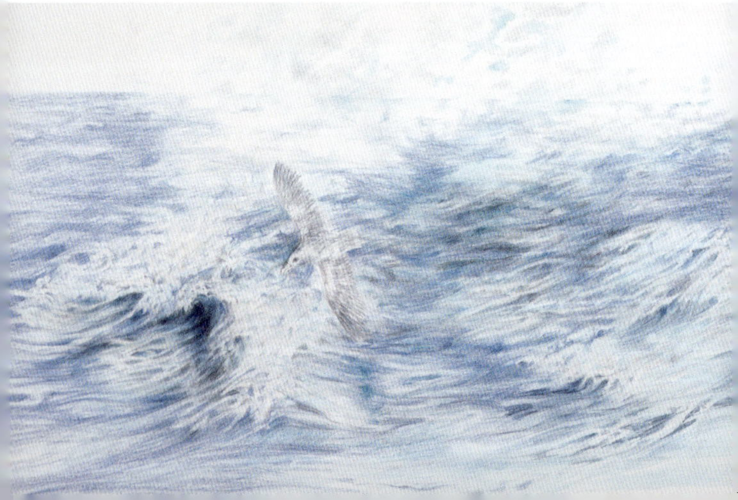

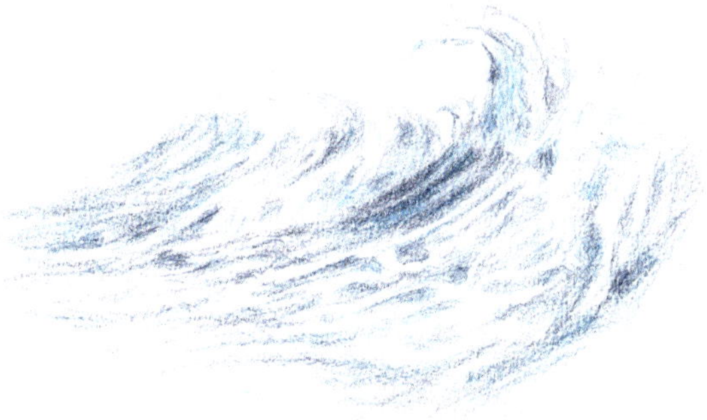

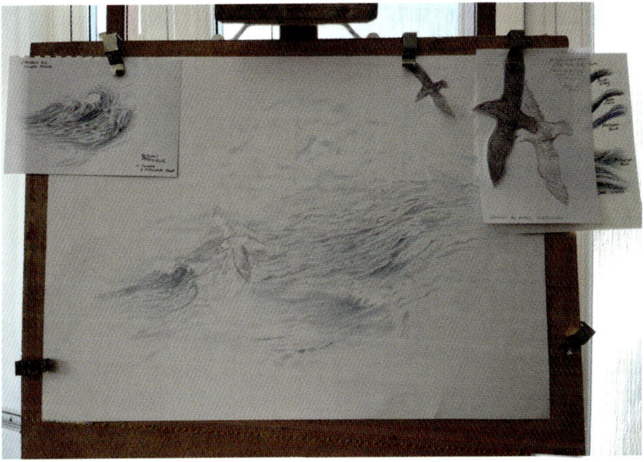

There is something satisfying in being able to pin elements of a drawing to a board to view in your own time. I often prepare work like this and leave it in view to think about. It helps me come up with ideas.

Adding Drama with Subtractive Drawing

Observing deer in a park, I realized that most of them were continuously grazing and when they did move, it was mostly with heads held low. I had visualized a different stance for my drawing, a majestic stag with its head held high! The light was dull and diffused so I waited, sketching the dark contrasting areas of negative space around the deer, until the sun suddenly and dramatically broke through, bathing a deer's antlers in light. Using a kneaded eraser, I removed graphite, adding form by creating a range of values of light and shade. In that moment, I had my composition.

I drew a few thumbnail sketches to work out the composition. The subject was the same but the focus varied.

1. I liked the design of this composition but was probably more interested when I drew the horns breaking the border.

2. In this composition, the pose of the deer with its head face on, causes the two front legs to be out of view with one horn lost against the body.

3. This was my favorite composition, which gave a clear view of the deer even though one horn is in front of the body. I decided to use charcoal, with a subtractive drawing technique to add emphasis to the horns by increasing contrast against a darker background. This composition favors the impact of contrast over details.

1

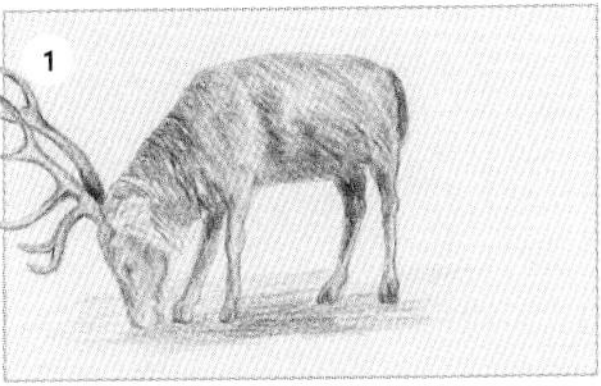

2

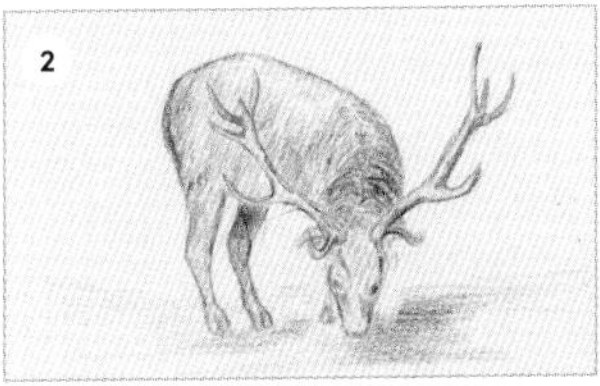

3

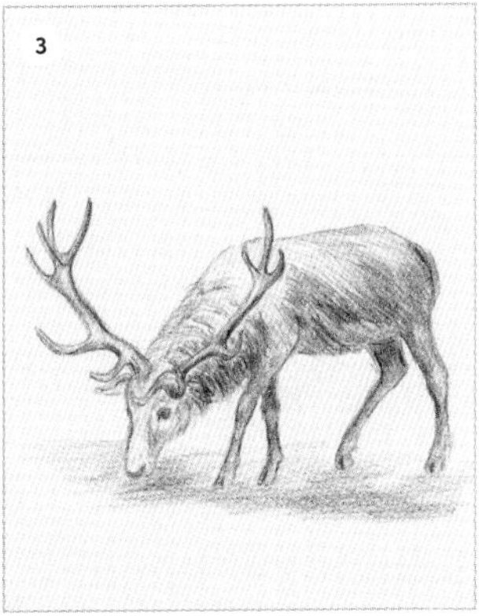

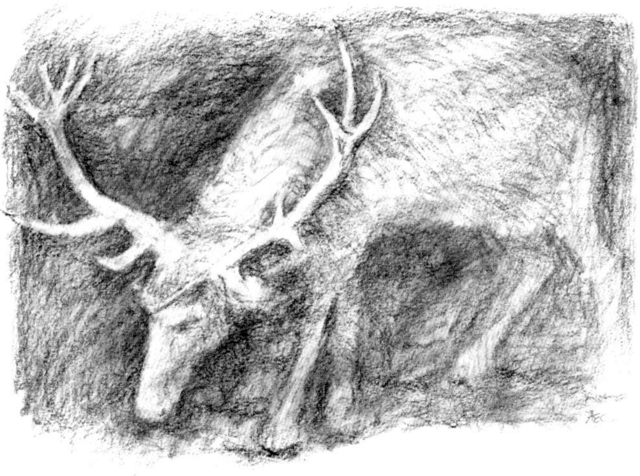

Imagination

Most people, if you ask them, will say they don't have much of an imagination and yet, isn't it the case that everyone has the ability to be imaginative but simply may not know how to recognize or use it?

You can use your imagination as part of the creative process in different ways. A simple example of this is if you are drawing on location but there is cloud cover on a gray day and you had hoped for a sunny scene in your artwork. If you have some of the elements you want to draw in front of you, make the rest up! Add a blue sky, reflections, and shadows from buildings and on the ground. With experience of sketching from life, this will become easier to do.

Trying to use your imagination when there is no visual reference is more difficult. I am often inspired by interesting light and shapes but that does not mean I know what to do with it. Ideas usually only come as a result of some effort,

To set the scene, I sketched this view of Venice from a distance. I used pencil with a light touch and then painted over it, on location, on the same day.

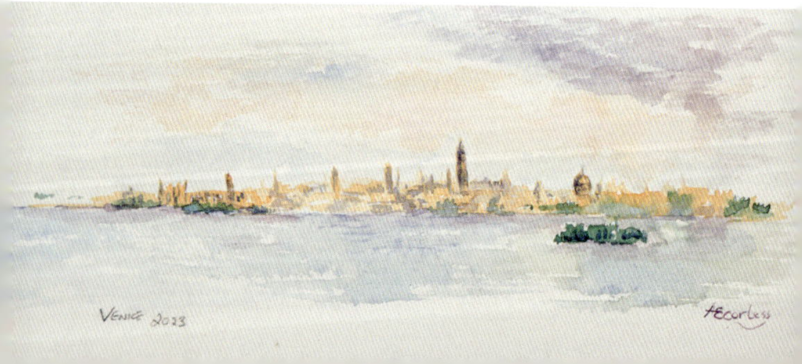

sketching elements that I want to include, and playing around with line and shape. I scribble, doodle, and draw little thumbnail sketches and then suddenly an idea for a composition hits me. Without this process, I'm stuck. I have to be drawing to come up with ideas and then I need to write them down straight away, or they may be gone.

My composition features different elements of this beautiful city that truly captured my imagination. To draw the cathedral, it required the use of perspective lines in the preparatory drawing. For the brass horse on the side of the gondola, I used comparative measuring and drew lines for references, measuring and comparing various distances with it.

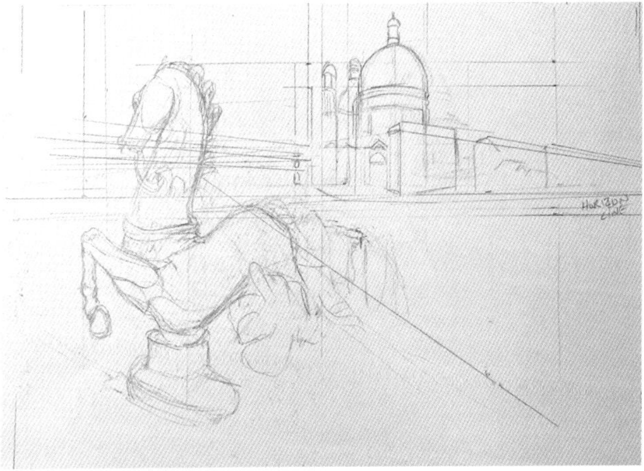

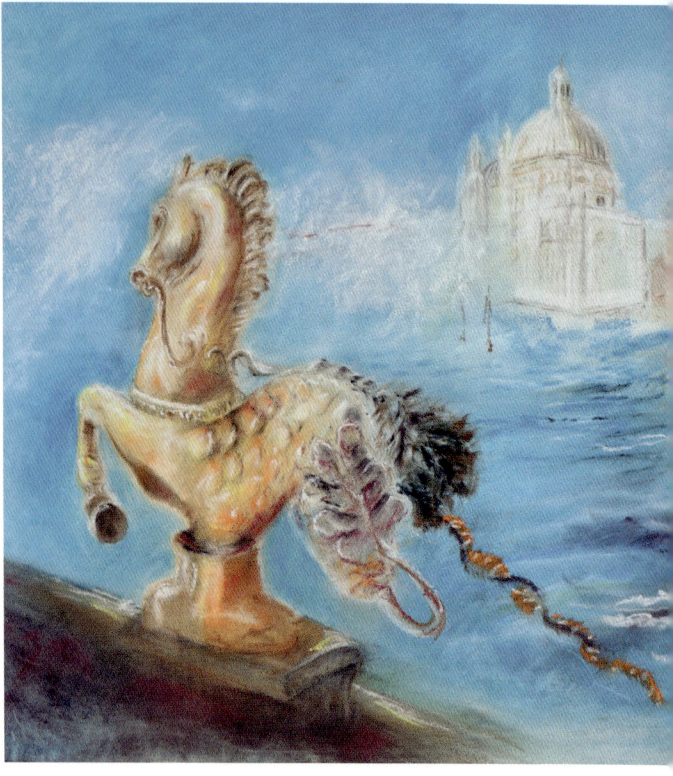

The focus of this pastel artwork is the interplay of the elements. The brass hippocampus takes on a reality as if it could escape from its base. The use of light is the feature of this piece, obscuring detail in some areas and adding a touch of magic.

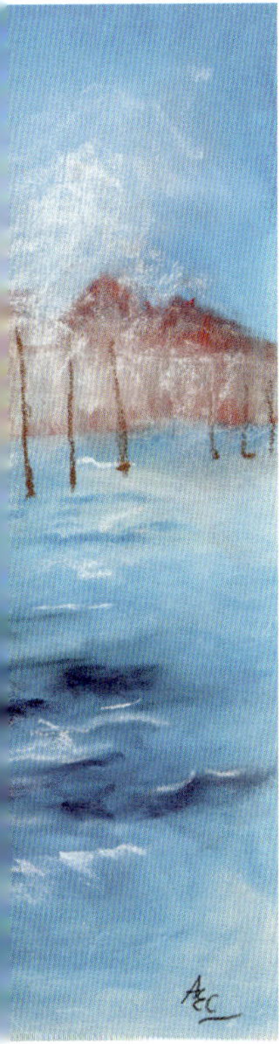

Putting it Together

Choosing compositional elements and making compositional decisions sometimes takes quite a bit of time, so think of it as an opportunity to explore and be creative, and don't rush. I often go back to old reference photos, videos, and sketches, enjoying a trip down memory lane, to see if I can put together elements for a composition.

For this pastel drawing, set in Venice, my focus is the brass hippocampus—a traditional ornament commonly seen holding the steering ropes on gondolas. Drawing this "sea horse" on a diagonal suggests movement. The placement of wooden poles on the opposite diagonal, as they mark the channel in the Grand Canal, adds interest. The large Basilica di Santa Maria della Salute in the background is partly obscured by sea mist, as are the other buildings. Adding mist, choppy waters, and only focusing on detail in the foreground, adds atmosphere and makes the hippocampus almost appear magical.

There is clear demarcation between the fore-, mid-, and background. It is the angles and perspective that are challenging. This is an imaginative artwork based on real elements.

CHAPTER 6

Color Theory

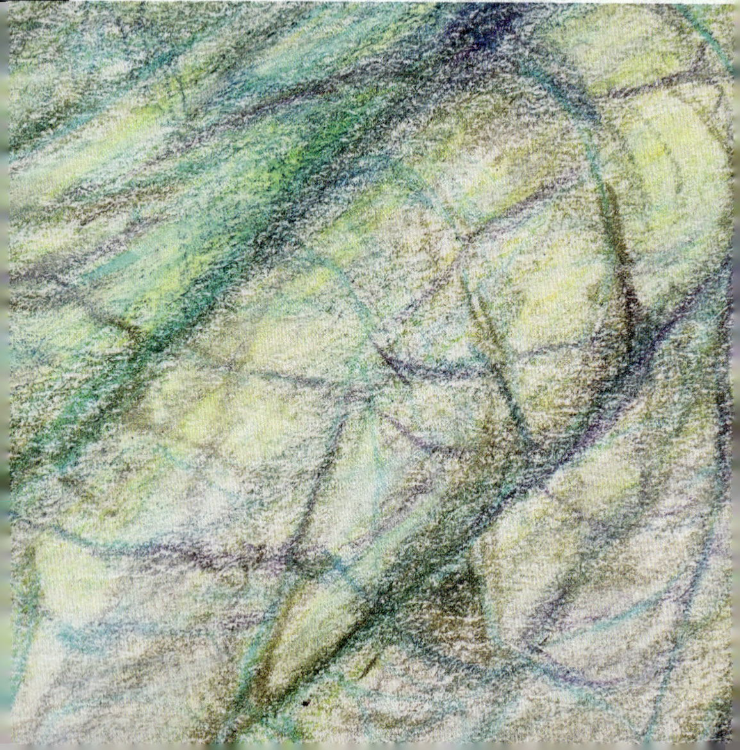

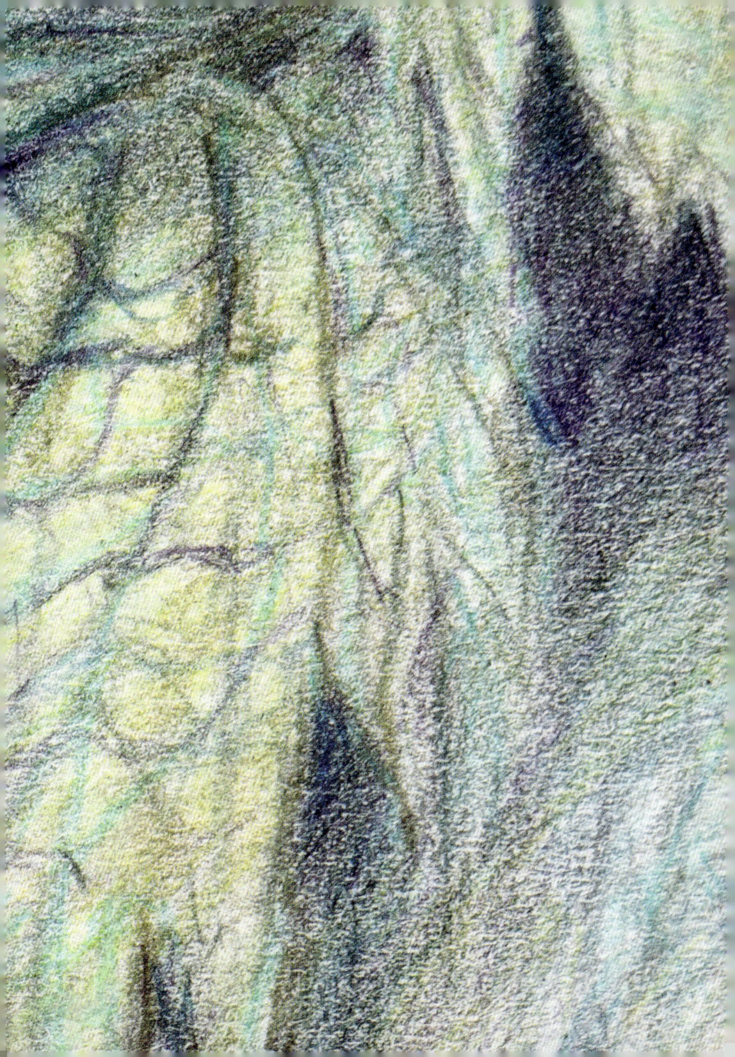

Exploring Color

Color theory is the study of how color is categorized, described, and applied using words and visuals. It is a subject that demands independent study because being able to apply the concepts of color theory to your artwork will give you an important set of tools for your creative practice.

Color Choices

Since Sir Isaac Newton first identified color with a prism and devised the color wheel (see Chapter 7), there have been numerous theories and developments in how to best organize color. Suffice to say that this book only gives an introduction to the topic. Whatever model you use, color, in its most basic sense, is described by its hue, value, and chroma (or saturation). These are the key components of color that I use in my artwork, but focus only on value when drawing with graphite.

Humans often have different perceptions of color. How we see color may be affected by adjacent colors. Colors are interpreted differently around the world and can signify different things. Color can cause emotional reactions such as feelings of joy, excitement, and fear, so you need to build color into your design choices.

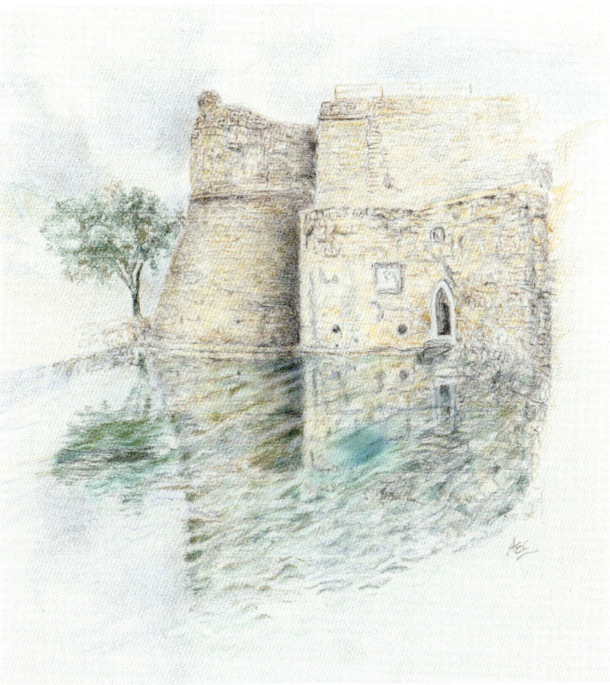

On occasion, a combination of elements, including color and texture, come together in a composition to give a truly magical feel. The artwork here is of the Gurdic Bastion Gate in Kotor, Montenegro. It would have been easy to overlook its green moat, colored by algae, as the sky from most angles was reflected in the moat, hiding the luminous color below.

How Color is Organized

So, how does it all work? Knowing how to identify colors and understanding the concepts of hue, value, chroma, and temperature is a good starting point in your color journey.

HUE

Hue is the name of a color. Red, yellow, and blue are primary colors because they cannot be mixed using other colors. Secondary colors are the result of mixing primary colors and are seen on a color wheel, which is useful with identifying colors. More on color mixing later!

VALUE

This refers to how light or dark a color is, and is sometimes called tonal value. Mixing a color with white creates a light value (called tints) and mixing a color with black creates a dark value (called shades).

CHROMA

Chroma means how saturated a color is, or how vivid it is. Achromatic colors, so called, have no chroma and are black, gray, and white. Achromatic or neutral grays are sometimes used to reduce the saturation of a color. Often color wheels show only highly saturated colors so choose one that also shows tints and shades.

TEMPERATURE

Color temperature separates hues into cool or warm colors. Warm colors (reds, oranges, yellows) lie opposite cool colors (blues, greens, violets) on the color wheel (see Chapter 7). In reality, it is sometimes difficult to tell if a color is warm or cool, particularly if their hue and value appears to shift due to a different adjacent color.

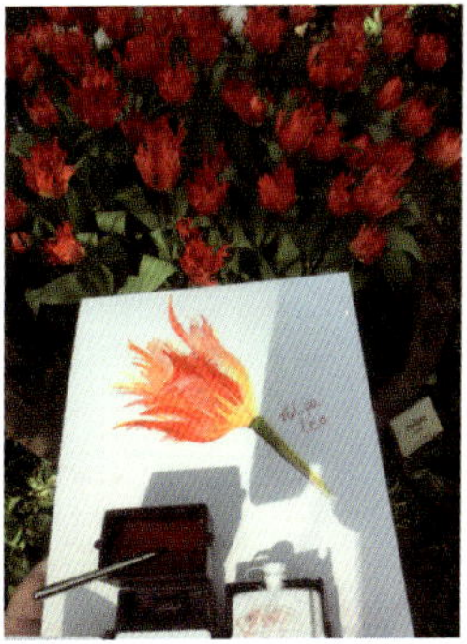

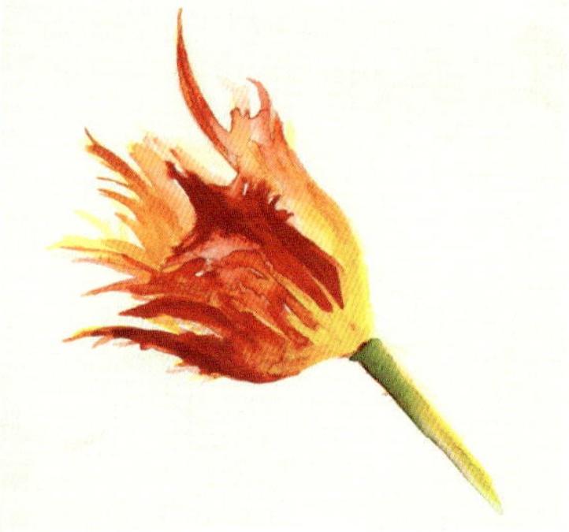

A watercolor painted from life at Gardens by the Bay in Singapore, captured the essence of the flower, the warm tones of the petals contrasting with the cool greens of the stems and leaves.

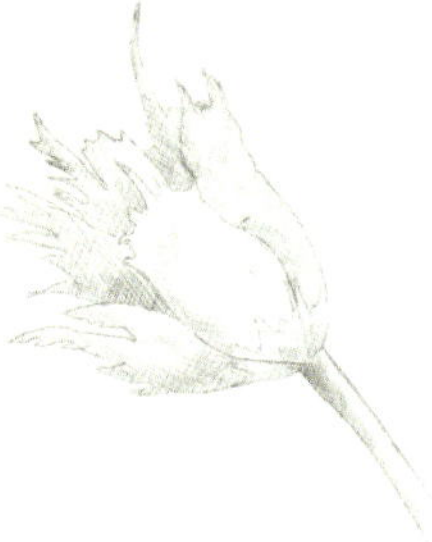

A sketch created back at the studio to work out values.

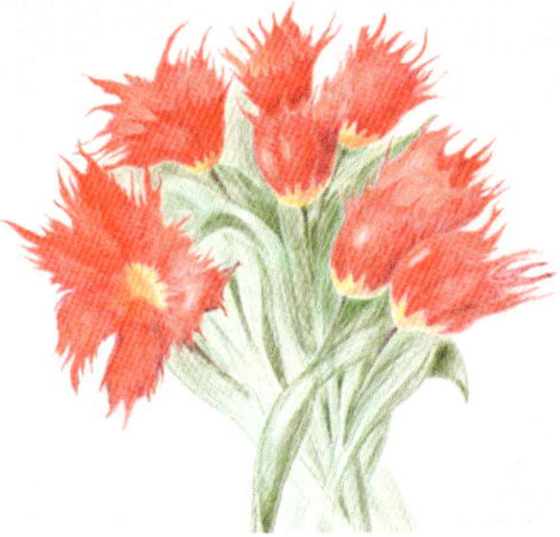

This drawing showcases the colorful petals against the dark green leaves, mixing colors to achieve darker values. A magenta over the yellow (in shadow areas) darkens the tone.

Is Color Accuracy Important?

Unless it is important for you to work to an exact color palette, why not think of your reference images as a source of inspiration, a starting point, and not necessarily something you have to copy. An important part of composition and color design is to decide on the suitability of the visual references you have and how you intend to use them. This is where drawing from life is more useful than trying to match colors of a photograph that may have been changed, sometimes intentionally in post-production by the photographer or by the printing process.

In this drawing, the butterfly is almost lost against the clouds, but by using imagination rather than recreating the color of the scene exactly, the butterfly becomes the focal point (see opposite).

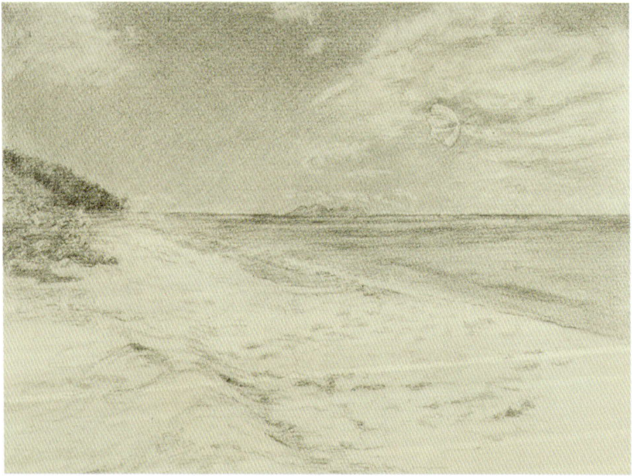

The artwork here was inspired by an experience of seeing the Great Southern White butterflies fluttering around beautiful beach areas of Antigua in the Caribbean, looking almost ethereal. I found out afterwards that not everyone had noticed the butterflies and yet there seemed to be so many of them. I wondered if my keen artist's eye had enabled me to observe my surroundings more closely.

I was excited to create artwork from our visit and my challenge became how to show the butterfly in its natural habitat. At first glace it looked like a cloud, so it needed some detail and a hint of color to distinguish it from the background. Hue and saturation were important but the bigger issue was value: which parts of the scene were lighter and which darker and where did the butterfly fit into that?

Watching the butterfly as it flitted past, it stood out, yet in the photos from our visit, it was almost lost. Using color on the butterfly, and adjusting background colors to create a contrast, makes it the feature of this drawing.

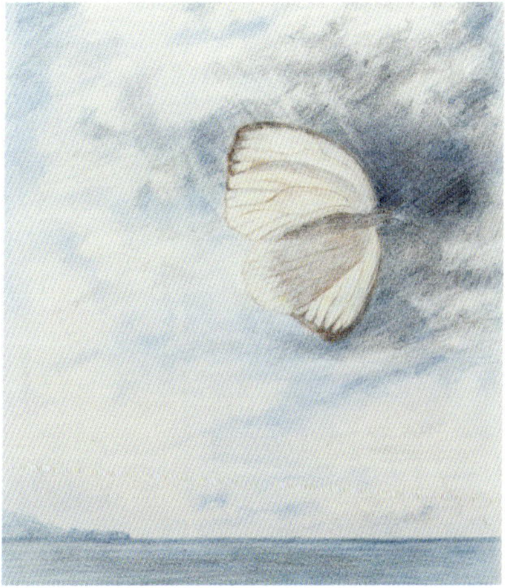

The Appearance of Color

When I drew the Royal Liver Building in Liverpool, it was bathed in the warm glow of a late afternoon sun, but it is still a granite-colored building. So what causes the color to look so different at different times? We perceive it as being different due to the light bouncing off it. The local (actual) color of the building is gray, from the gray granite façade, but the quality of the daylight and atmosphere changes how it appears, sometimes quite dramatically.

When drawing with graphite, it is possible to show these changes. When there is neutral diffused light, such as with light cloud cover, the building would have no strong shadows but in the late afternoon sun on a bright day there are reflections (highlights) and strong elongated shadow shapes to draw.

Learn to observe color in different lights. When the light is bright, colors will look more vivid, an observation that came from my earliest experiences as a child growing up in countries around the world.

The famous Liver birds on top of the towers, their wings half unfurled, reflect the light and stand out against any sky. The scene is always magical.

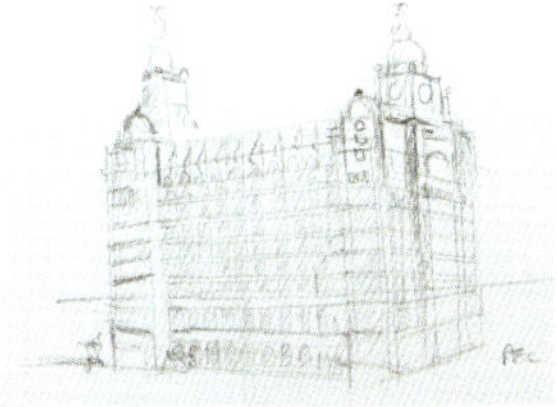

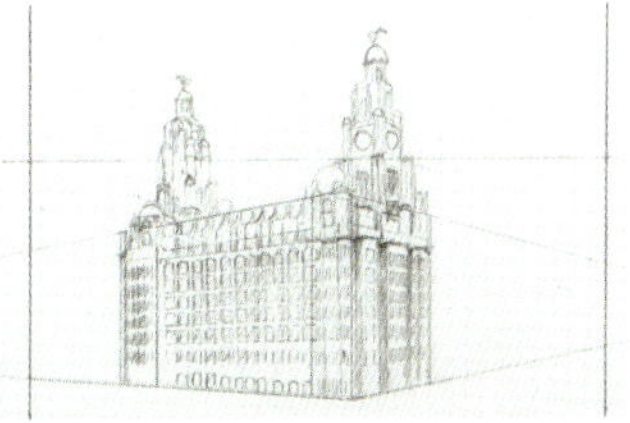

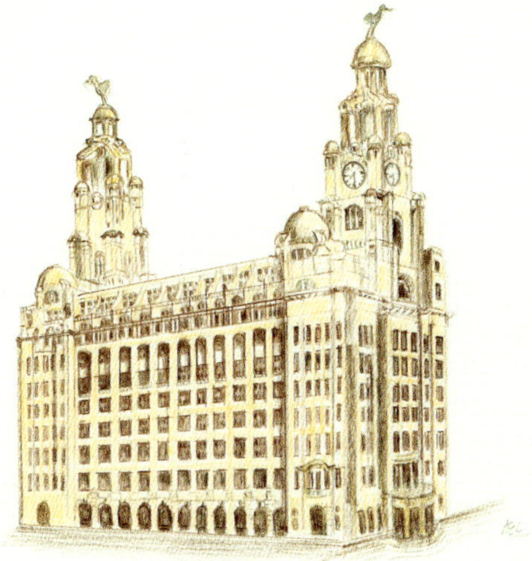

Unless there is a reason to render accurate color in a drawing, remember that color changes dependent on lighting and atmospheric conditions. It is more about getting the value right. Color is a choice.

Working in Monochrome

Working in monochrome, or working with one color, is often interpreted as having to work with black and its tints and shades that graphite pencil or charcoal produce. However, working in monochrome means working with any single color you like!

If you are new at working with color, choose one to explore and enjoy drawing a range of tints and shades. It is a useful exercise in understanding how color is interpreted as value and for this reason, I often suggest using a monochrome color as a next step after working with an achromatic color (having no color, such as black or white).

As with working in full color, remember to draw a few thumbnails to use as an aid to remember things, such as identifying where the light source is and what the composition is. Try making your own value scale in your chosen color, from light to dark.

Without the luxury of a full color palette, you can add interest by employing a number of different techniques. Try working with extreme contrasts of light and dark. Consider adding textured marks. Design an interesting composition where the focus is on the placement of elements, and color doesn't make much difference to the final artwork.

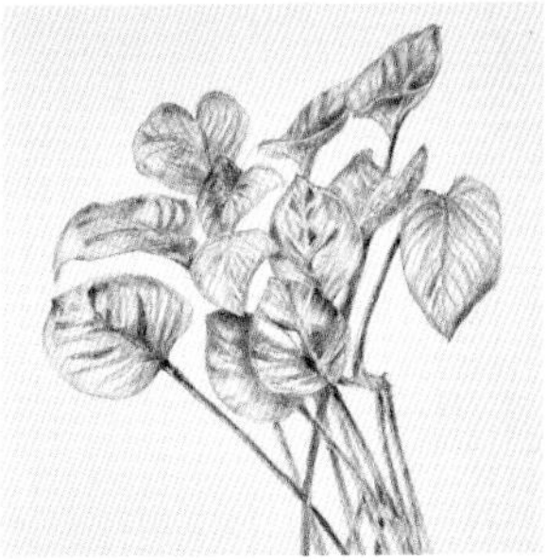

Working in monochrome using a single green pencil still allows the lights, midtones and darks to be seen which is how the drawing is given form.

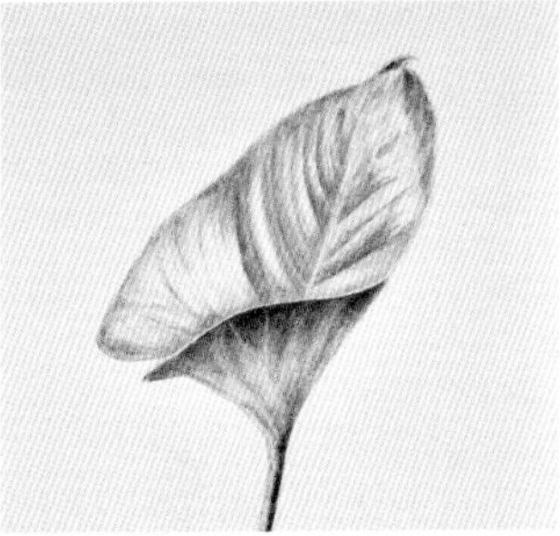

A closeup of a leaf shows how working in monochrome allows the focus to be on the value (the lights and darks) without being confused by color.

I saw this plant during a visit to Singapore. It really did not need much definition or any color as the interesting shape was the focus. In the drawings above, the shapes were lost within the group, so creating contrasts working with one color, added interest.

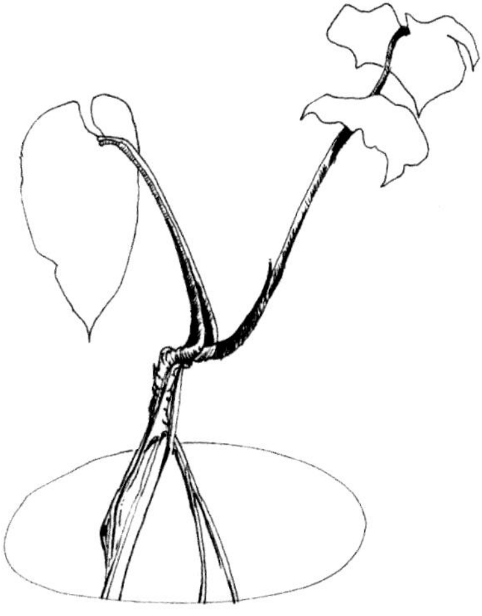

Working with Color

Color gives you an extra creative tool, which makes it easier to identify different elements of a drawing. It adds mood and atmosphere, and can signify meaning. Having worked in monotone, you should now have a good understanding of tonal value, so before you start your drawing, try creating a value scale of some of the colors you intend to use. This will give you an understanding of the lights, mid-tones, and darks you can achieve. Keep assessing the values of your colors, the drawing will work best if the values are correct.

Try photographing your artwork with your phone and convert it into grayscale. Does the drawing still work or are some of the values too similar? Do you need to change them or add an additional color?

Experiment with complementary colors (colors positioned opposite on the color wheel) and research the various color models available for artists. There are quite a few!

When drawing the macaws in color, only a simple composition is needed because the color itself is interesting enough. When drawing the birds with graphite pencil, it becomes clear that there is limited tonal range in the feathers and so the composition becomes more important. Without color, there has to be something visually interesting in the artwork.

To humans with trichromatic vision of red, green, and blue (RGB) these parrots are wonderful to see.

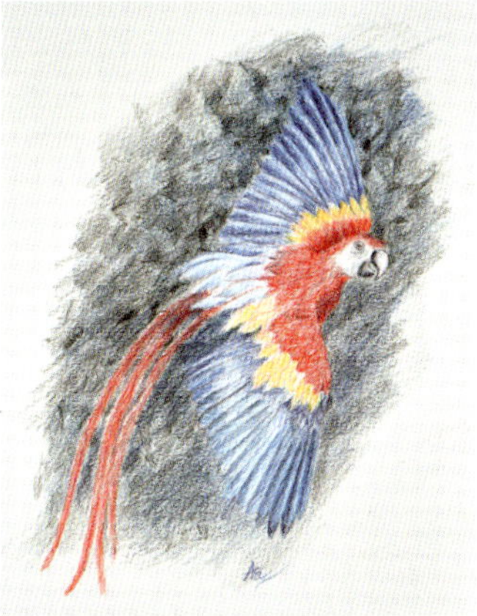

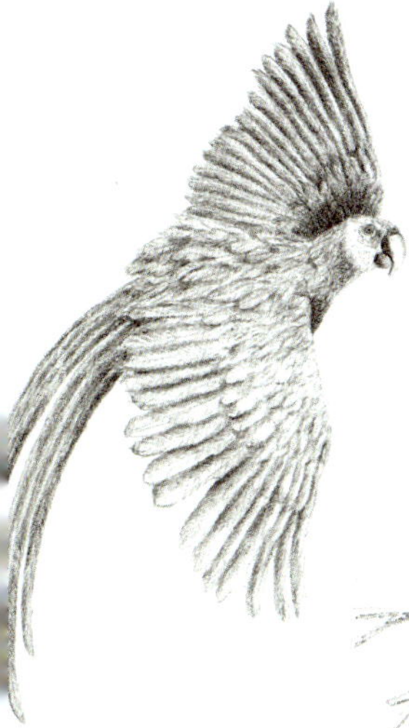

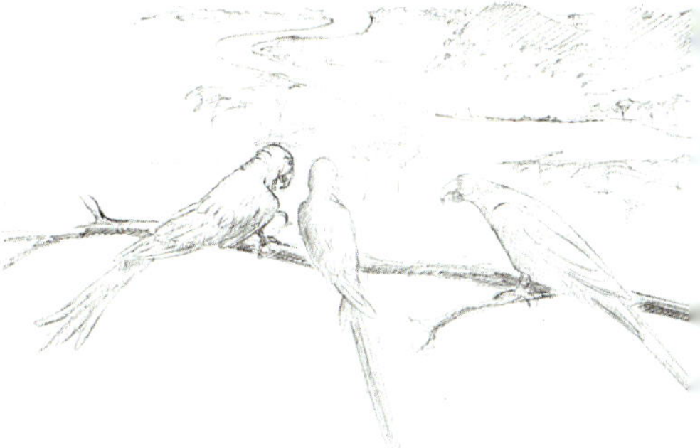

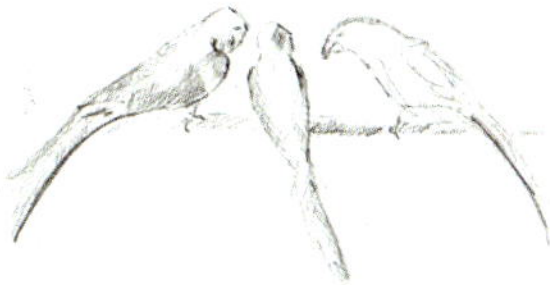

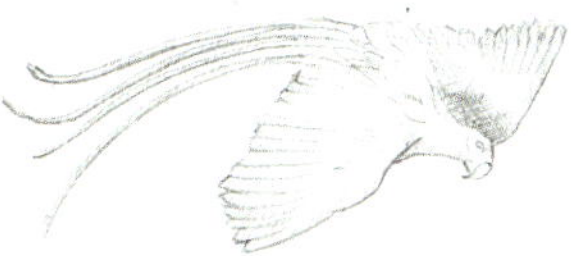

CHAPTER 7

Color Mixing

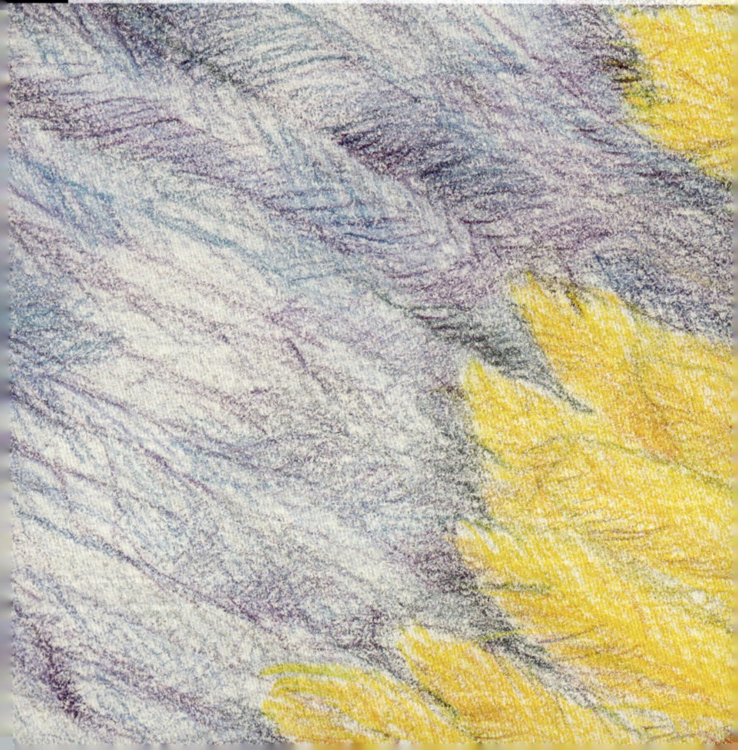

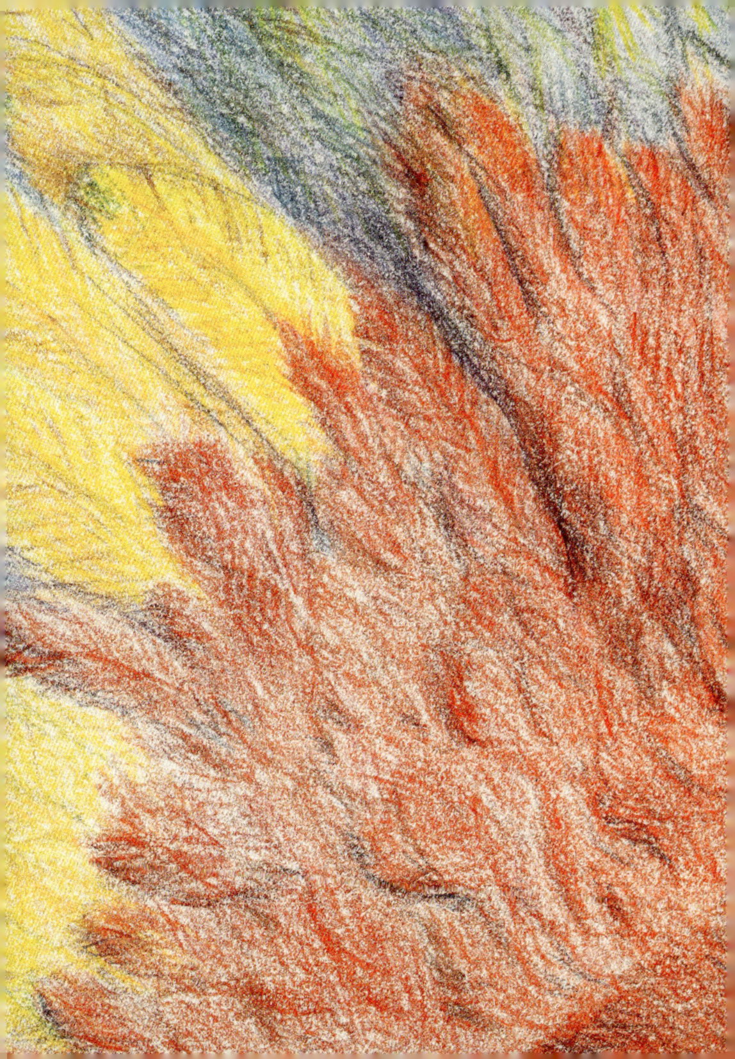

Creating Colors

The use of color has to be an accurate color match in some genres, such as botanical illustration, where color mixing is usually carefully worked out and recorded. For many other types of artwork, color and color mixing can be an extra creative tool that allows the introduction of different elements.

In tonal artwork, where there is a gradient of tonal value, colors have tints and shades. In watercolor, adding different amounts of water affects how light or dark a color looks. Without the vehicle of a fluid medium, different approaches are needed with dry media, although some pencil artists employ a fluid medium in their work. In all other cases, wet media colors are mixed away from the paper, in a color palette. Dry media is usually mixed on the paper.

Color mixing is a time to play with color. Results are not always what you expect!

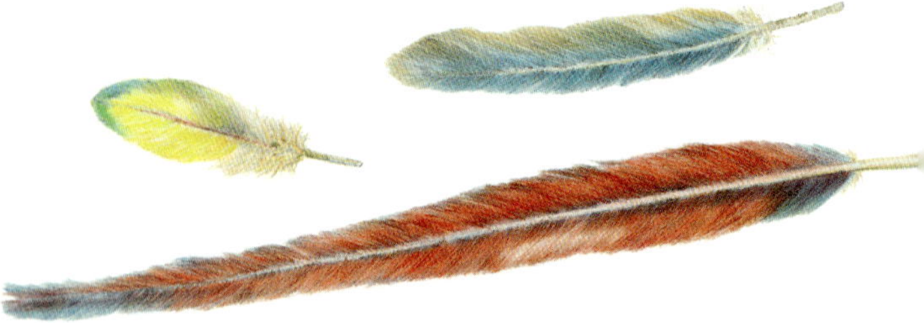

Layering

Colored pencils are often layered and blended by going over marks with another color, hatching and cross hatching. Sometimes a scumbling technique is used. This involves drawing small circles of color gently onto a paper, so as not to flatten down or burnish the paper. Different colors can be laid next to or gently over each other.

Pastels are usually mixed on the drawing surface. Remember, pastels will not adhere well to a smooth surface, making it almost impossible to layer different colors on top. A paper with tooth will hold the pastel and may even result in unexpected effects when layering other colors on top.

Tinted charcoal pencils enable bold expressive marks with a touch of muted color, which can also be layered. Pen and ink can be layered using a pen (hatching and cross hatching) and a brush.

A Note on Safety

Keep safety considerations in mind when mixing colors. There may be more dust created so be aware of this when working with charcoal and pastels. Ensure you have adequate ventilation, consider wearing a mask, and perhaps gloves. Mixed media use might include paint so remember to check paint labels. Some paints are toxic.

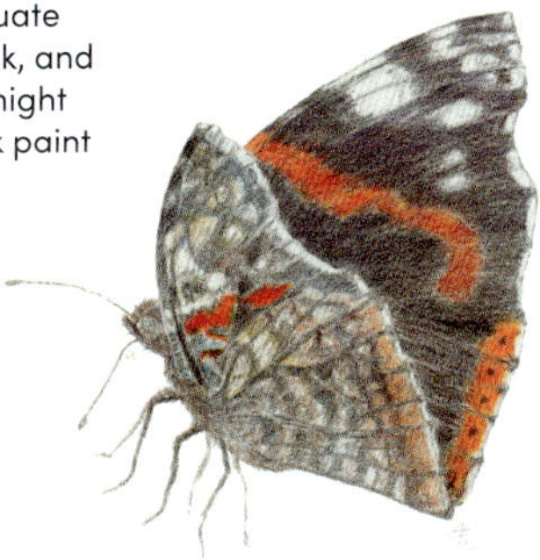

Mixing

It is not always possible to find the exact colors you need for a drawing. Luckily, most colors can be mixed. Be aware that, although this is true for many types of art materials, there could be an unexpected problem if you mix products from different manufacturers. This is due to the different amounts of fillers and binders used in the manufacturing process. Different makes of colored pencils and crayons can also have different color biases, and so will skew any attempts at color mixing. Consider color mixing part of your creative process to be kept in your visual reference library.

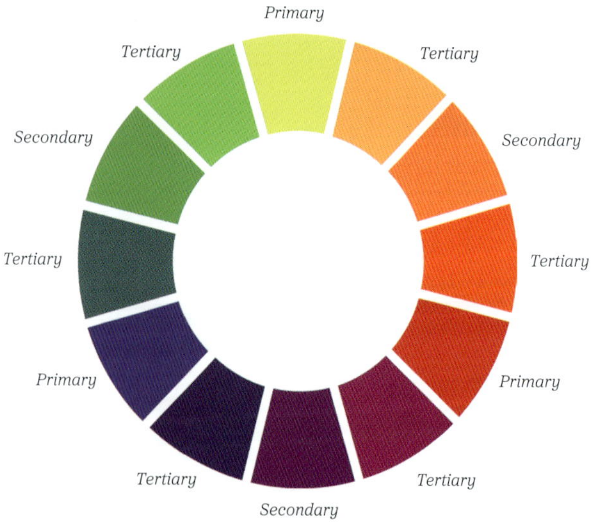

THE COLOR WHEEL

Using the color wheel as a guide is a good way to start practicing color mixing. The primary colors of red, yellow, and blue can be mixed to make secondary colors of orange (red + yellow), green (yellow + blue), and violet (red + blue).

Secondary colors can be mixed to make tertiary colors, which sit in between the primary and secondary colors, for example, red-orange sits between red and orange and yellow-orange sits between orange and yellow.

If you need contrast, choose a complementary color situated directly opposite on the color wheel, or choose a split complementary color (situated either side but next to the complementary color). There are a number of different color schemes and it is worth researching and exploring all of them as part of your journey.

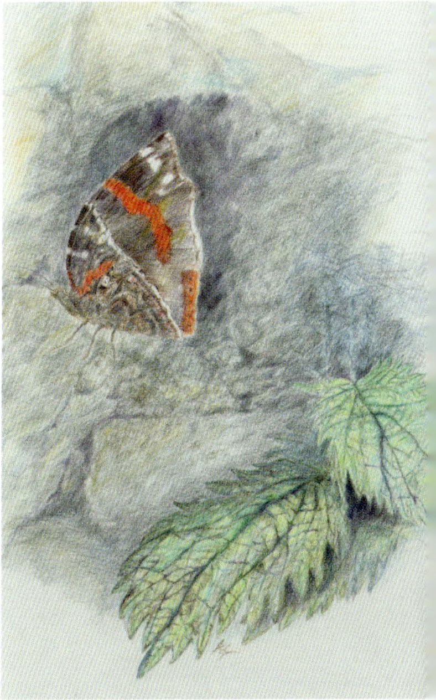

The red admiral butterfly has wings of red (primary color) and orange (secondary color). The hue of the stones is gray but the value changes, depending on lighting conditions.

Sunsets and Light Waves

The intensity of hues seen in this Caribbean sunset are from the scattering of blue light waves. They are intensified by the longer path the light travels through the atmosphere at both sunrise and sunset, which the longer wavelengths of red, orange, and yellow are able to penetrate.

Notice how the blues and the oranges are opposite on the color wheel, creating a complementary color scheme. I began the rendering (creating the final drawing) of the artwork from scratch. There were no thumbnails, no preliminary drawings, just an almost instinctive response to a scribbled sketch done shortly after the sunset, and a video and photos. I encourage you to draw what you see, to respond to colors that capture your imagination.

This first tonal sketch of the sunset shows the same intensity of light as the pastel drawing in color. The same long lines of light fall on the water and as the sun rapidly disappears, the land becomes silhouetted against the strong light, losing all detail.

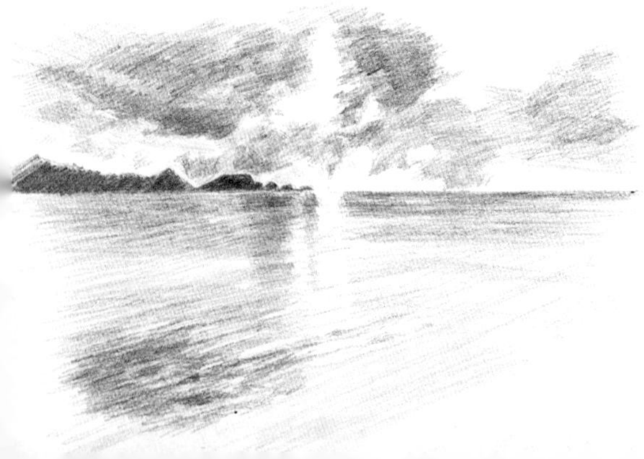

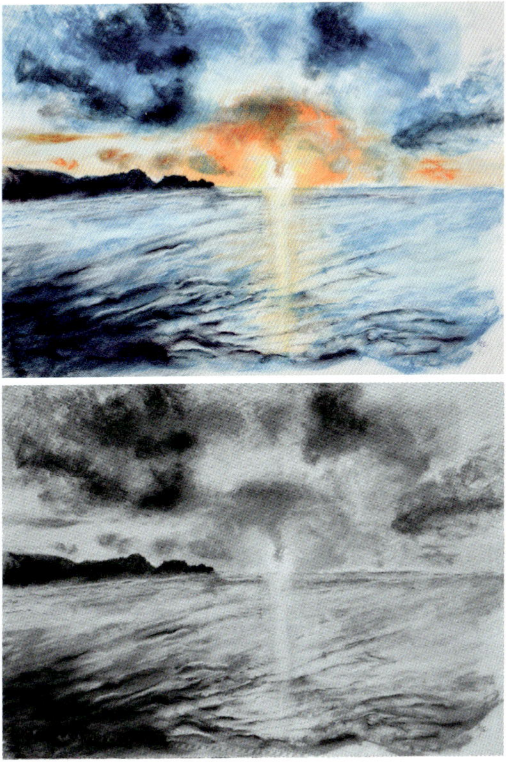

The focal area of the drawing was the colors and the intensity of light. Drawn again in color in the studio, this is how I remember the scene. Using soft pastel colors has given extra choices which come out stronger when desaturated, than the original quick pencil study.

TRY THIS: COLOR SWATCHES

Make your own color swatches and label them. Make them large enough to compare to other swatches. Note the manufacturer's name, as art materials of the same or similar names can vary in quality.

It is always important to make a note of colors used, no matter what the medium, because if an image works, then you may want to use those colors again.

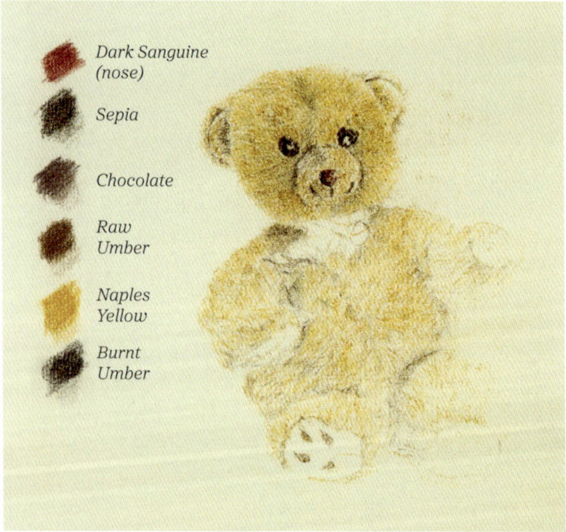

Artist Insight

Whether in a pencil or paint, pigments need a binder or medium to hold particles together. The graphite in pencils is often mixed with gum Arabic as a binder, sourced from the Acacia tree. When drawing, the graphite can be heard scratching over the paper as it is deposited. When the first pencils were manufactured by Derwent in 1832, artists had a medium they could easily transport. It was the smoothness of prepared graphite and its resistance to heat that resulted in it being widely used in the industry.

With the introduction of paint tubes, albeit collapsible at first in 1841, artists were able to transport art and paint more easily outdoors. Oil painters used mediums such as refined linseed oil, turpentine, and other driers. Before this, paint was stored in glass containers or pouches, kept in an artist's studio.

Before the invention of pencils, paint pigments were mixed with a concoction of mediums. In the Altamira cave paintings in Spain, there is evidence that raw earth pigments were mixed with animal fats. Egg tempera, a mixture of egg, pigment, and oils was a popular medium at the time of Leonardo Da Vinci (1452–1519).

CHAPTER 8

Start Your Drawing

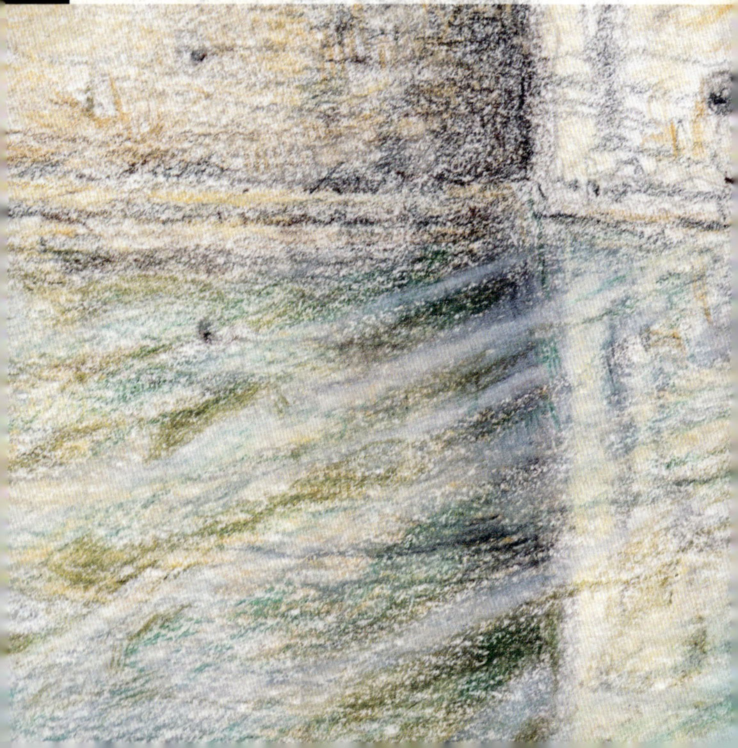

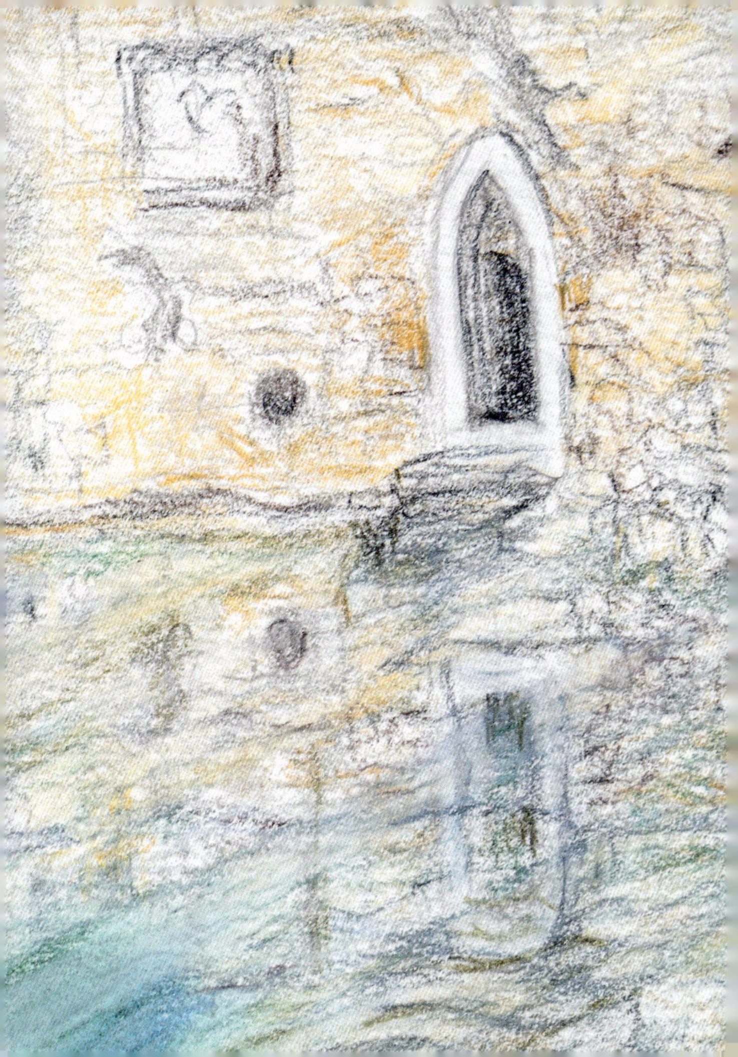

Making Your First Marks

When inspiration strikes, it's much easier to start a drawing if you follow a tried-and-trusted workflow. Creative decisions are best made before starting on an artwork, to allow for most eventualities. Planning includes deciding on a subject and identifying the aim of the artwork, working out what visual (or other) references are needed, sourcing art materials, and working to a timeline. A good creative practice allows for spontaneity in your work. It is also something to rely on when things get challenging. Learn to trust your creative practice.

Work Through Your Checklist

We looked at forming a creative process at the start of Chapter 2, based on four questions. Ask yourself those questions now. What is the artwork for? What materials do you have? What reference images do you need (if any)? How much time is available? Don't forget spare paper for practice marks and any notes. Spontaneity is much easier to achieve if you always plan ahead and are prepared!

Always consider your personal safety and wellbeing. Are you using anything noxious or flammable in your artwork? Do you have adequate ventilation in your creative space? Have you considered fire safety and is there an accessible exit route?

Allow time and space for your creativity and, after all this, even if you draw the most simple piece of art, you have had a successful creative experience. Sign and date everything you draw and never throw it away. With experience, you can start to self critique and after gaining confidence, consider joining a group. Seeing how other artists approach their art and creative issues is a valuable experience in your creative journey.

I had not done any research or planning before visiting the beautiful City Hall in Belfast. A quick internet check confirmed there was no problem drawing it. The chosen position, requiring two-point perspective, was made for me as that was the view from the only bench available to sit on! I chose this view rather than lean on the front gates to draw a one-point perspective view.

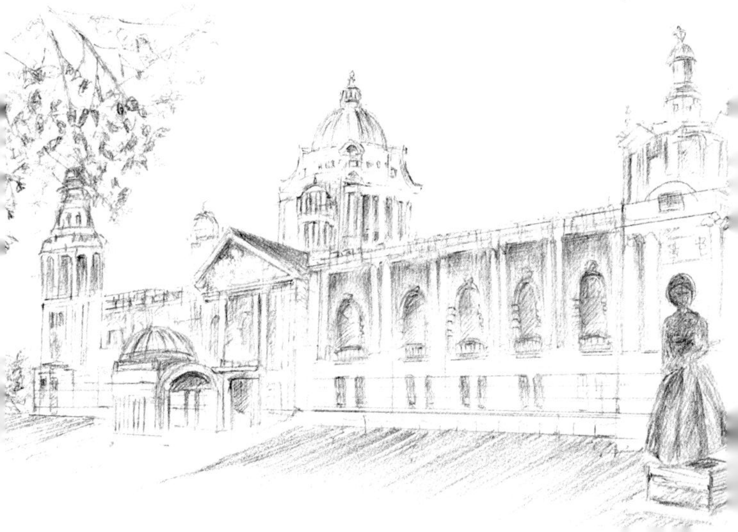

Creating Form

Drawing animals from life is an opportunity to learn more about form and function, observing movement, weight, and balance. However, when the shape is covered by a heavy double coat, as with a Highland cow, it is not so easy to see.

Start by drawing cylinder shapes for the neck and body. Add a cone for the head and develop the drawing from these basic shapes. If anatomical landmarks are not visible, focus on other elements.

Drawing like this does not have to be about finished artworks, they can be enjoyable exercises to capture different angles and poses. For precision, draw with a pencil. For a more expressive feel, draw with charcoal.

The pose of the Highland cow in the initial preparatory drawing and in the final rendered pencil drawing is the same, and yet there is far more intensity in the final artwork.

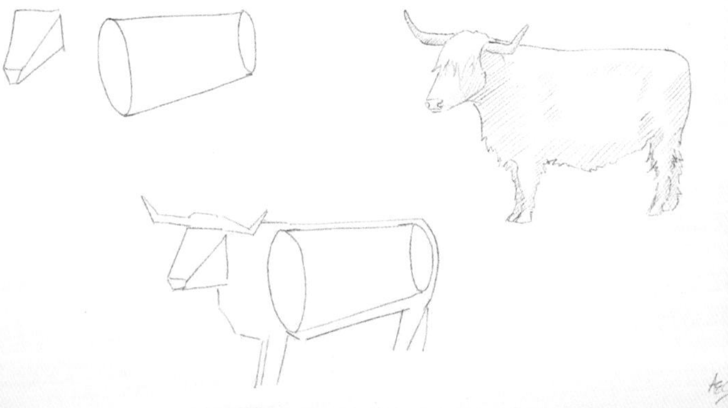

The pronounced shading and use of highlights on the horns leads the eye to the sharp tips, giving the onlooker a sense of wariness that is just not there in the initial drawing. The slightly turned head, with hair moving across the face suggesting recent sudden movement, and an intent stare from the barely noticeable eye, is almost a warning.

All these gestures are apparent from a still image and are created by giving the impression of size, force, awareness, and movement, all from careful use of light and dark, texture and shape.

Whatever your subject, try drawing simple shapes first to give the artwork form, rather than drawing an outline with no supporting shapes to guide you.

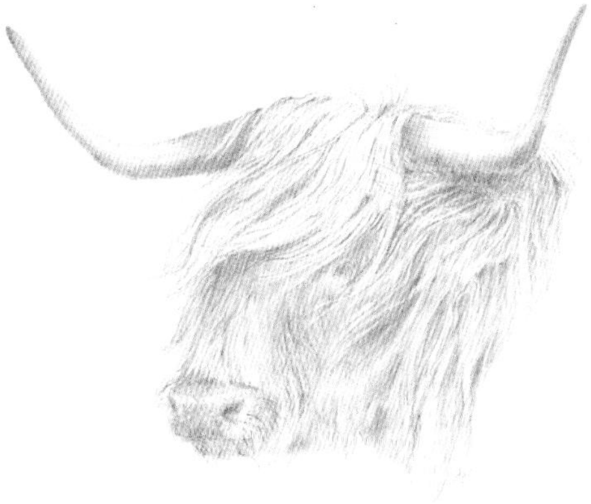

Drawing on Location

When preparing to draw outdoors, it is important to consider issues such as whether you need permission to draw and if the environment is safe. Are there any hazards? Do you need permission to be there or to create artwork of your chosen subject? This is especially important when drawing people such as when urban sketching. Consider if you really need to draw recognizable features.

There is a joy in drawing on location. For me, it's the only way to really observe and take in the world around me.

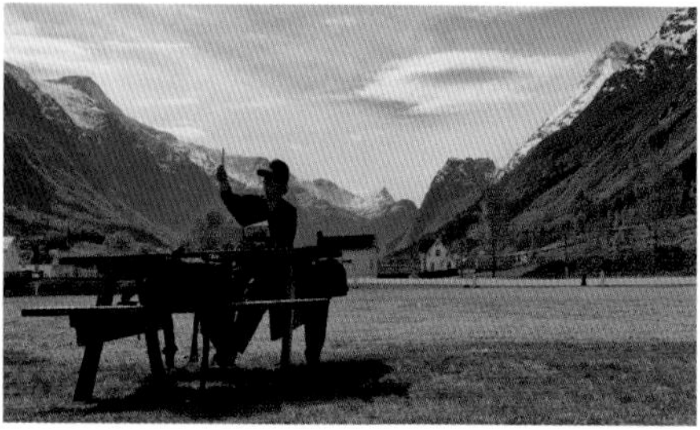

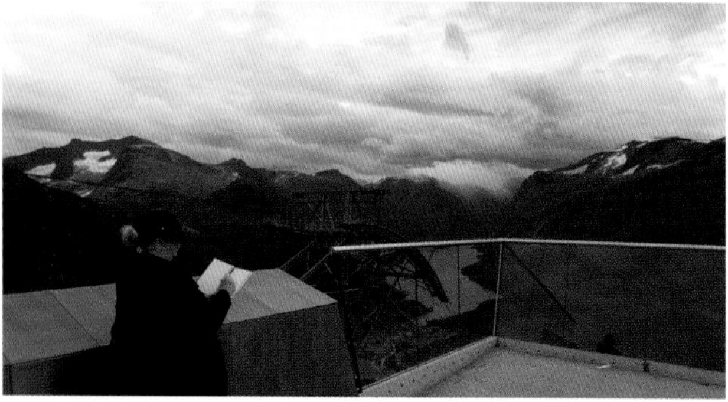

USING SKETCHBOOKS

Small sketchbooks are easy to carry around and fun to use. My sketches are references for any future projects I may decide to progress. More importantly, sketching makes me take the time to observe my surroundings. I am inspired by the natural world and, whenever possible, I try and capture scenes and images on paper. It's a good habit to keep a sketchbook on hand as it is easier to make a range of marks on quality paper. I also like to carry a sketchbook clip to keep the sketchbook closed in transit. Sometimes, my sketches are jottings and ideas but if there is time, I like to work directly from life and take time to observe the scene.

I like using different types of sketchbook but my favorites are those that open flat.

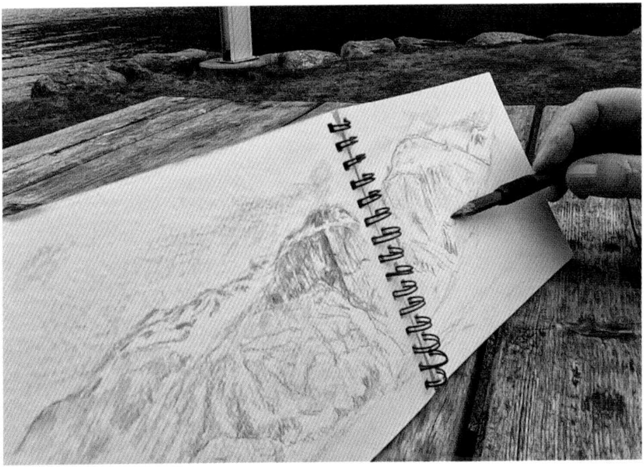

OBSERVATIONAL DRAWING

Drawing on location means dealing with other factors such as changes in light and weather conditions, which can make it difficult to hold a sketchbook steady. I wait for the best light and capture what I see, reinforcing marks quickly. If the light changes or the view is obscured by weather conditions, I still work on those first impressions, adding further marks as I can.

Nature journaling, or field sketching, are ways to record nature, and the action of stopping to observe is key. Always make a note of the location, the time, and the weather. It is easier to work on a composition at a later stage if you have all the visual information you need.

You may be surprised how working on location trains you to quickly make decisions about the most important things to include in your drawing. This sketch of a Northern Fulmar, as seen in Chapter 5, shows the acute angle of the body and wings as it skims the waves. Little detail is needed and, with the bird flying at speed, there was limited time to capture what I needed.

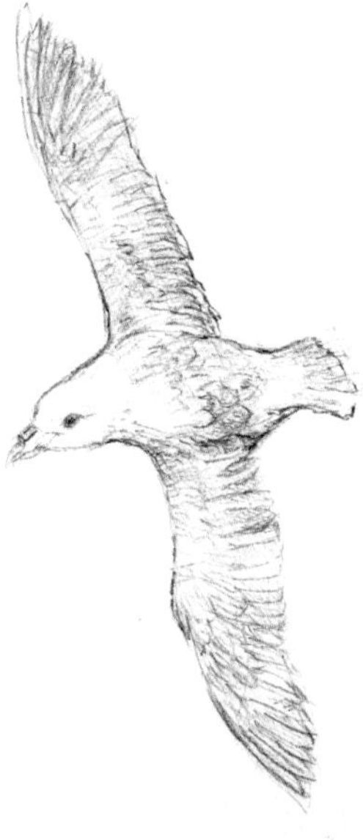

FINALIZING THE ARTWORK

Back in the studio, I am able to assess what I've drawn on location. This artwork started life as a sketch done on my trip to Norway. Pencil marks can be clearly seen as I used the side of the pencil to apply tone to the sky and the mountains. This is a reference drawing so it really doesn't matter that these lines are visible. What is more important to me is that I captured the values (lights and darks), the shapes, planes, texture, and some detail. A little more work was needed to clean up the highlights.

The aim here was to capture the magnificence of the mountains rather than any elements in the foreground.

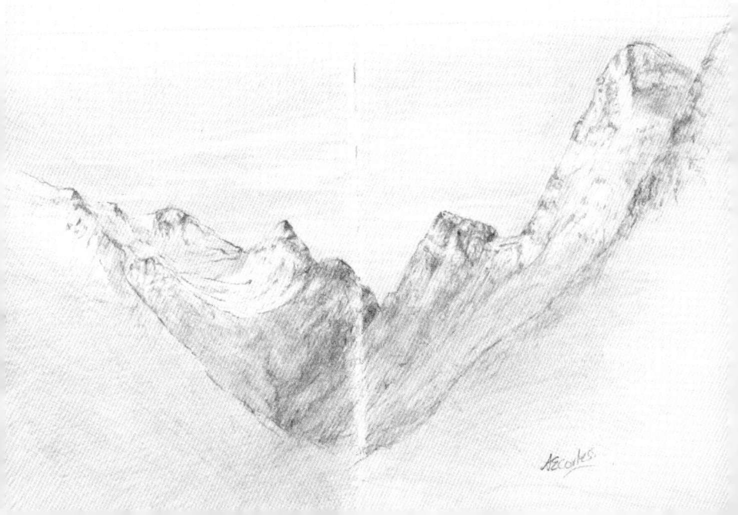

Researching to Add Narrative

My style as an artist is to create artwork that has narrative. I like to have a focus, a story to tell, so it is not just the visual image that catches my interest. Sometimes, the story is there to see, such as the owl drawing in an urban setting (in Chapter 3), which says nature is never far away.

As a keen wildlife artist, I love researching animals. When I first saw a clouded leopard (in Chapter 3), I had no idea about its unique anatomical characteristics, such as ankles that rotate to allow for a headfirst descent from trees. I created a sketch to remind myself to include this in future compositions. When I researched the scarlet macaws (in Chapters 6 and 10), I discovered that they live high up in the canopy of forests, rarely descending to the ground. My final image in Chapter 10 shows a macaw flying high above a forest canopy with a river far below. The composition takes account of this behavioral feature of these birds.

I love drawing elephants and have observed African elephants in the wild many times. I am less familiar with Asian elephants and so my drawings are to record their anatomical features. I then imagined an Asian elephant chomping through bamboo, a key food source, in the wild. Without any actual reference for this image, I had fun and made it more abstract and quite colorful!

This Asian elephant artwork is at the exploratory stage in a sketchbook. I enjoy creating detailed artwork but it is also fun to create more abstract marks, suggesting shapes and movement.

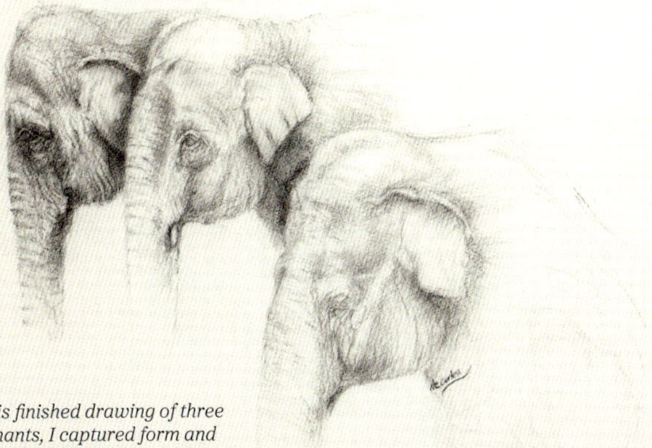

In this finished drawing of three elephants, I captured form and expression. I created the work to become more familiar with the Asian elephant and to add to my own visual library.

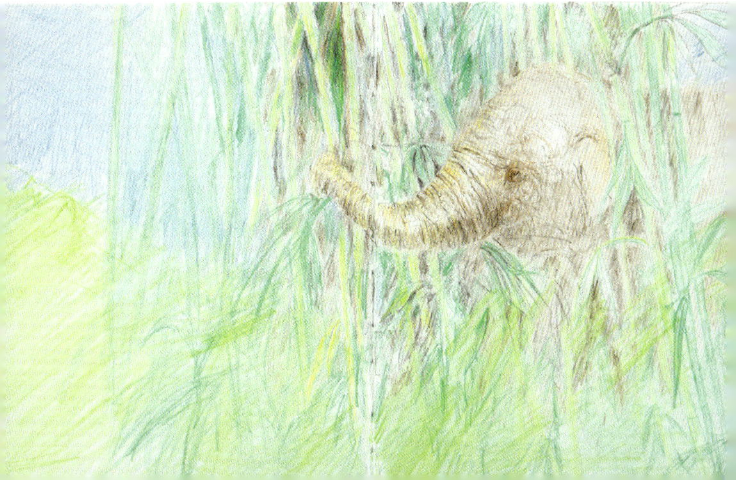

Be Inspired by Light and Movement

I am inspired by the natural world and, whenever possible, I try to capture these scenes and images on paper. Often, it's a quality of light that catches my interest, such as reflections off water, dramatic rays of light falling onto landscapes, or a backlit view. When movement is involved, the subject becomes even more interesting. In these drawings, sharply angled lines broke up the rectangular shaped cave entrance, reflecting shafts of light. It was made more dramatic by the rolling sea below and the flashes of light, as kittiwake birds flew in and out at different angles at speed.

When capturing images outside, remember to use glassine paper or similar to protect your drawings in a sketchbook and use a clip to keep it closed. Working outdoors invariably means coping with different weather conditions, so protect your drawings.

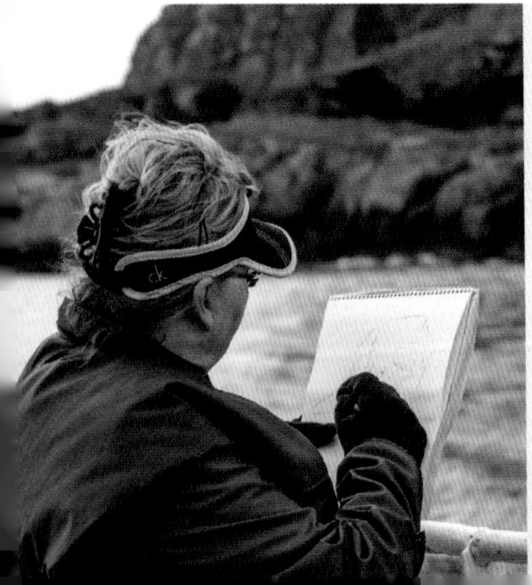

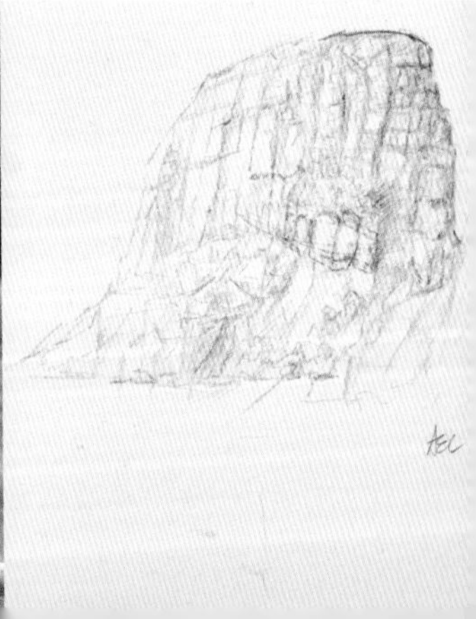

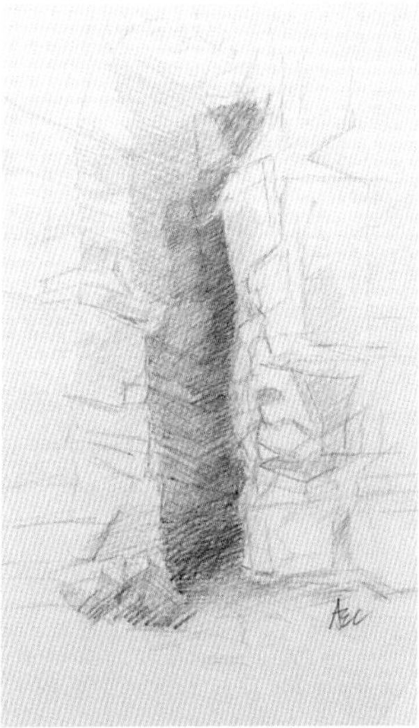

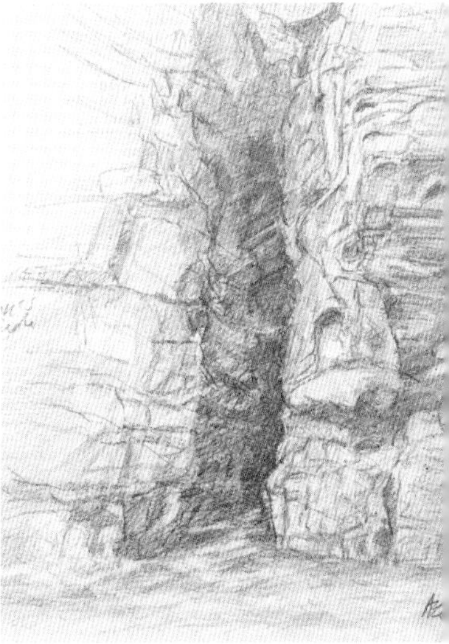

Natural history subjects that are of great interest to me are sometimes difficult to find, often due to their location. With limited time, and dependent on weather conditions, I work quickly. I liken it to writing in shorthand. My mark making might appear untidy and as soon as I am able, I try to make more sense of it by adding more detail or re-drawing. These drawings are precious as they are my own unique visual information.

DEVELOPING NEW IDEAS FROM OLD

My research for the cave drawing (on the previous page) gave me ideas. The kittiwake birds appear to scatter at speed when exiting the cave. There was a reason for this. White tailed eagles circle the island, high in the sky. With their visual acuity, they can see the dark feathers of the kittiwakes against the sea, but less so if angled and moving rapidly. The rolling sea was adding to the drama, as it crashed into the cave. In contrast, nesting kittiwakes were perched on improbably small rock ledges with fledglings. My focus for the drawing was to show the chaos, speed, and sanctuary.

In this version of the cave, there is a more abstract feel. You have to look for the kittiwake birds, who are constantly at risk from the eagles high above, so they fly in to the nesting chicks at speed, and at extreme angles. Safety in numbers!

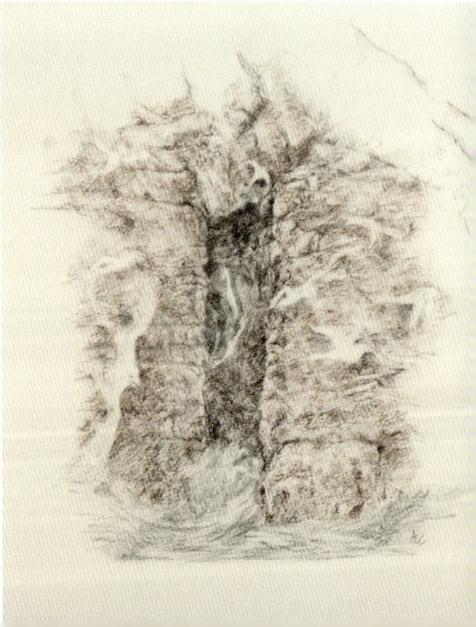

TRY THIS: REVIEWING YOUR OWN WORK

During a project, it is a good idea to allow time to assess your artwork. You will probably have worked on your drawing in the same place and position, so put it somewhere different and allow time for reflection. Look at the artwork from time to time but separate yourself from it by working on something else.

There are different ways to get "another view" of your drawing. Take a photo of your artwork and view it at a smaller scale, convert it to grayscale, and see if the values work, or look at the artwork in a mirror for a reverse view.

You could also write a few notes about the artwork, such as what the aim of it is (you might have done this before starting the artwork) and what the main area of interest should be. Then come back to the artwork later to see if you have actually achieved your goals. It may not matter if you haven't, but it is a good reminder that if you like your artwork to have purpose and focus, then it is worth taking time to review it.

CHAPTER 9

Build Your Drawing

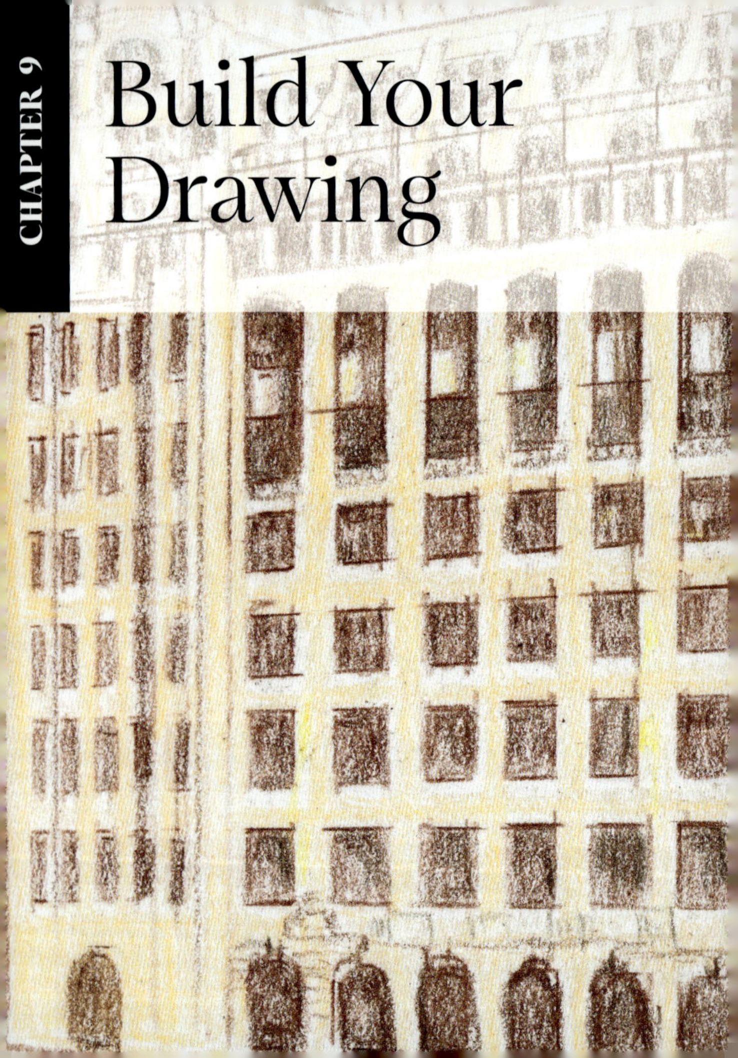

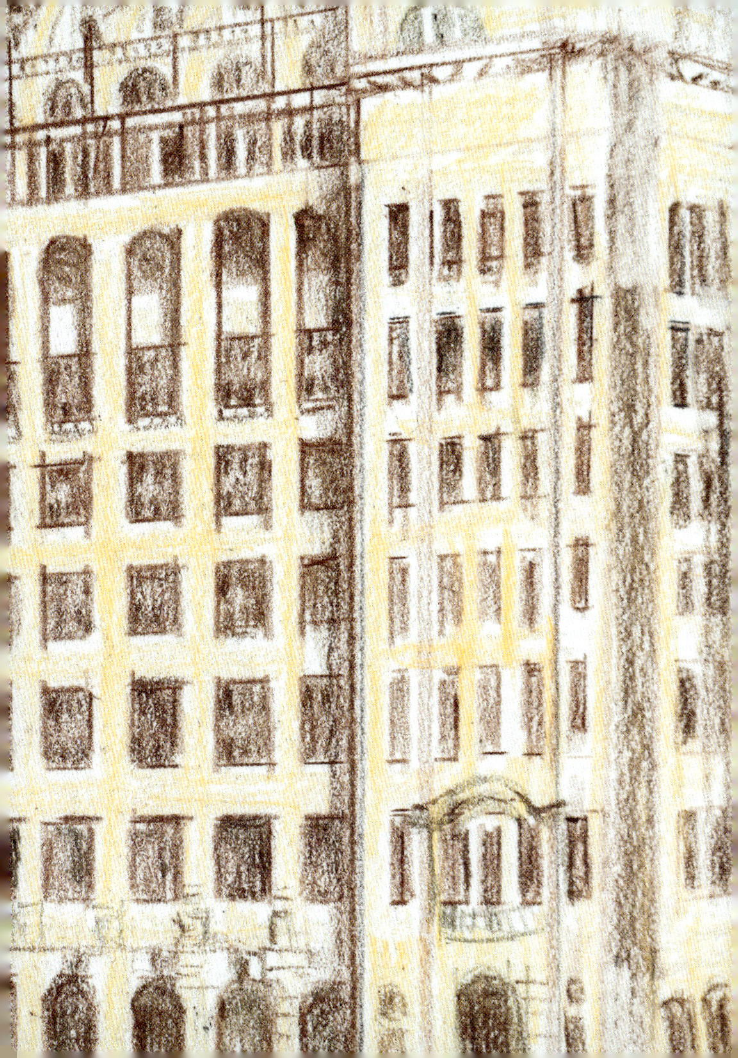

Developing Your Work

When working on a project, it is useful to regularly pause and ask yourself some questions. Have you got the right subject? Are you focusing on the correct elements? Are you using the correct art materials? It is also important to make sure that all the elements of composition have been included. It is often not too late to make changes or corrections.

My Process

As a guide, here's the process I use, but you should do what works for you.

- I always build a drawing up gradually across the surface using my thumbnail drawing as a guide. If I have spent time working out the composition with a preliminary drawing, then I rely on that instead, and try not to get caught up looking at photographic references.
- Once I have drawn out the composition, sometimes with very few marks, I identify where my dark and light value areas will be, leaving the lighter areas mostly untouched. I tend not to lay down a mid-tone all across the paper. I prefer the surface to reflect light in highlighted areas with little or no tone applied to interfere.

- My thumbnail might be my guide and I will have planned what media to use, but I usually wait until the drawing is at this stage before making rendering decisions. I like to start feeling a connection to my artwork and I work through this initial exploratory stage, getting used to the bigger size, the feel of the medium, and the paper. If it's all working, then usually the drawing progresses quite fast. It does not always go smoothly.
- I find my artwork goes through an untidy stage, where I can lose my original drawing marks, resulting in a delay as I try and get back to my thumbnail drawing guidelines.

This sketch of Asian elephants, each one drawn separately but on the same sketchbook sheet, helped me form the idea for the final artwork in Chapter 8.

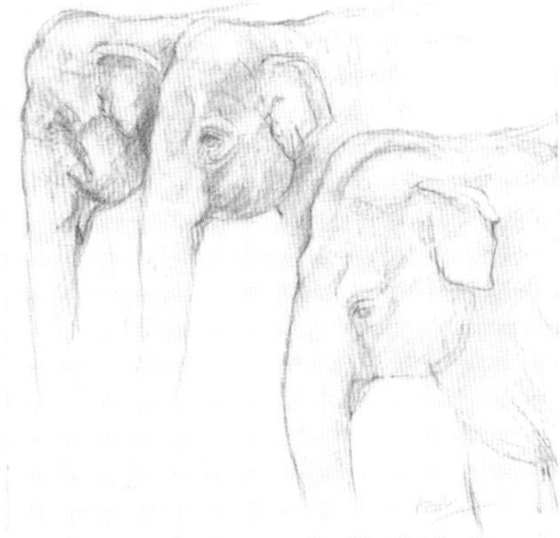

Beacon Fell Walk-Through

Let me take you through how I created this image of Beacon Fell in Lancashire. On a recent trip, butterflies flitted around stone walls, foxgloves lined the pathways, and when I started sketching the view from the top, I said out loud that all I needed was a bird of prey. Then someone shouted and pointed at a kestrel, high in the sky. All afternoon, we were treated to an exhibition of the bird hunting, its wings beating rapidly, scanning the ground for prey. It was a wonderful sketching opportunity, except that the kestrel was sometimes just too far away, making it difficult to draw. I had to rely on short bursts of observation when it flew nearby.

Looking over the beautiful Lancashire countryside to Beacon Fell in the distance (on the left). A butterfly flutters in and around the hedgerow. Sketched on location with a soft 4B graphite pencil.

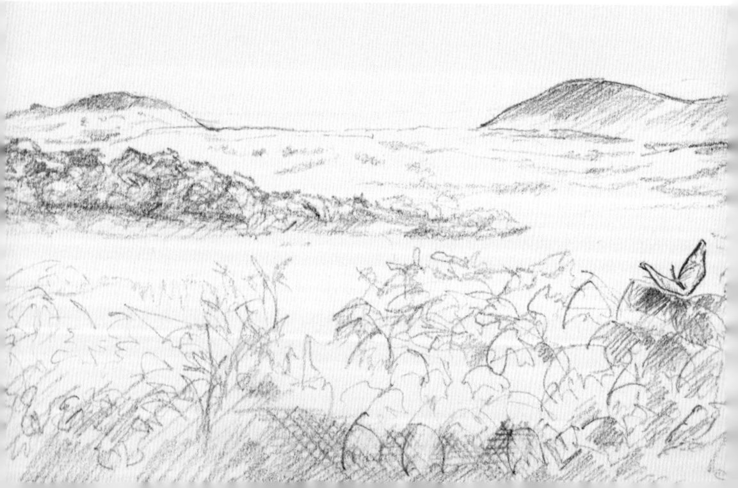

STICKING WITH MY PROCESS

Drawing from life, and having to work within the dimensions of a sketchbook, has made me focus more on design (it has to fit on the page). Back in the studio, I almost did not do any thumbnail value studies as I was confident that I could remember the view and lighting conditions. I then reminded myself that I should stick to my creative process to review and assess and I am glad I did. It gave me the creative space to realize that although my main drawing was ready to be copied and rendered, at some point, I would create more separate pieces of artwork from the day, namely of the kestrel, the butterfly, and the foxgloves.

Working from life gave me so much visual information that I was able to move quickly from the sketches to the final composition.

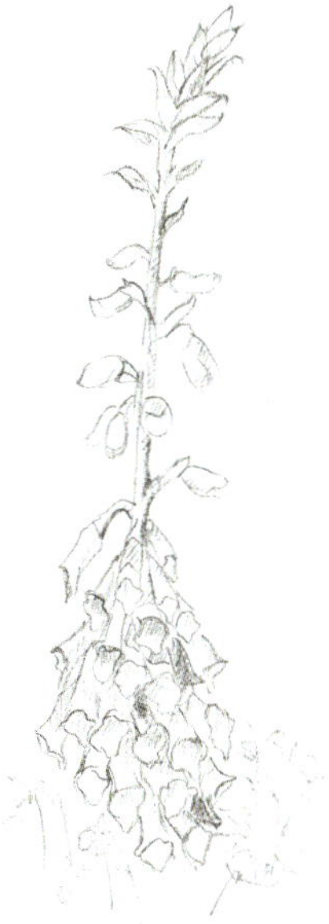

Purple and pink foxgloves grow in clusters with spikes supporting the bell-shaped flowers.

Using a small sketchbook makes it easy to manage drawing in windy conditions.

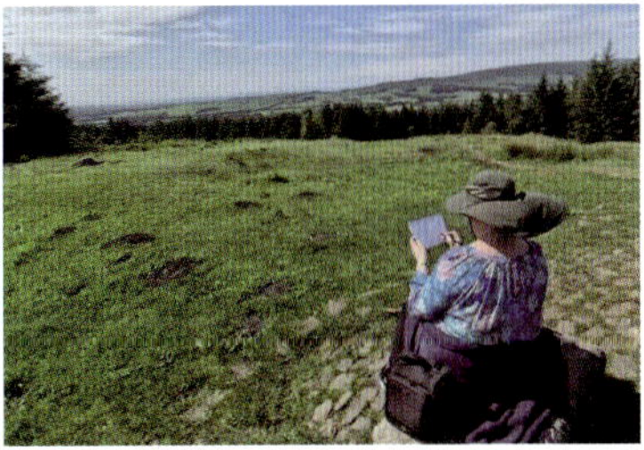

DISTANCE AND AERIAL PERSPECTIVE

The distant mountains appeared blue, caused by short blue light waves being scattered. With graphite, it is possible to suggest this effect with faint pencil marks and soft edges. The use of this atmospheric, or aerial, perspective is a useful device to add depth.

Working with a small sketchbook means drawing a smaller image than I would like so I place the important elements first to ensure it all fits!

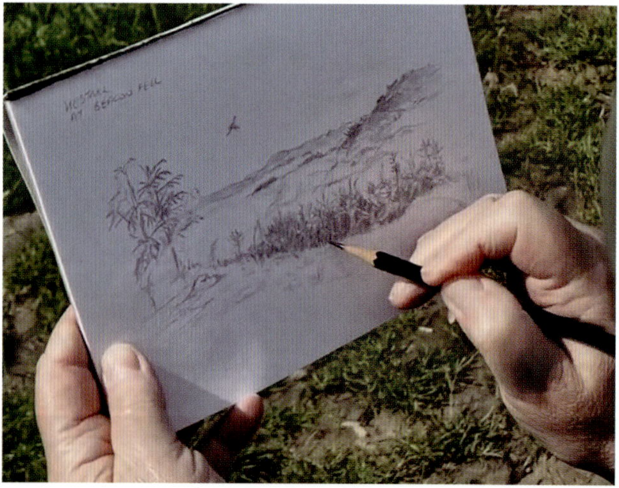

A hunting kestrel hovers, with its head steady, when looking for prey. I tried to capture the different angles of the head and noticed how the wings and tail feathers were used to maintain the position. Sketched with an HB graphite pencil.

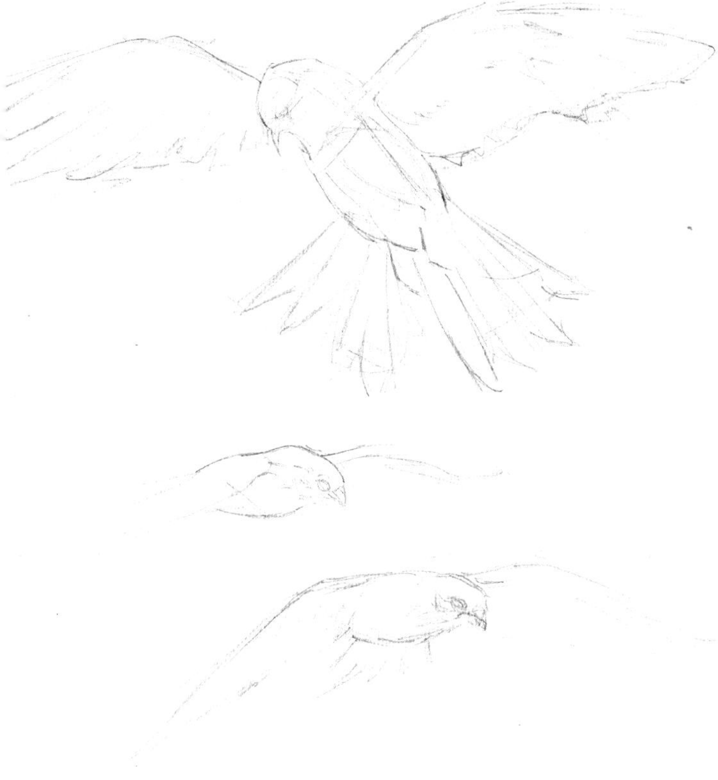

DEVELOP YOUR SKILLS

It is often worth re-examining visual references to see what other artwork can be created from them. It is also worth using opportunities such as this for development of creative skills. For example, I made a short video of the day, recording some of the drawing on location.

This drawing splits into foreground, mid-ground, and background, and is a good exercise in landscape drawing, as it contains the elements seen and encountered, sometimes unexpectedly so. This has become part of my visual library.

Sometimes, there is no need to improve on a drawing done on location. Even though it is in a sketchbook, this graphite sketch is a complete artwork that captures distance and atmosphere, and is a reminder of a wonderful family day out.

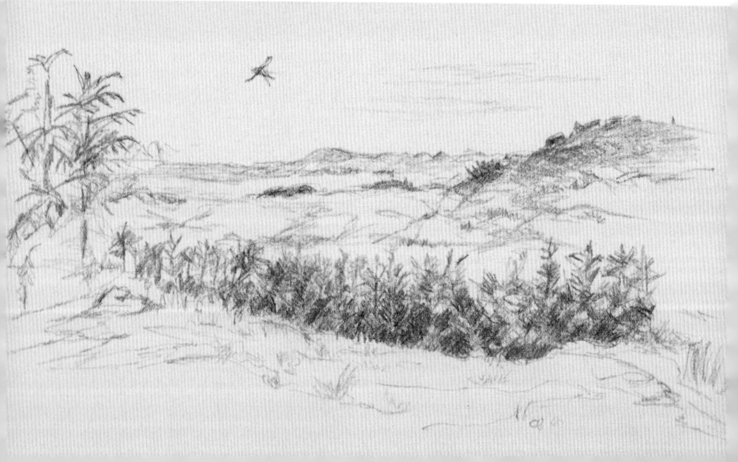

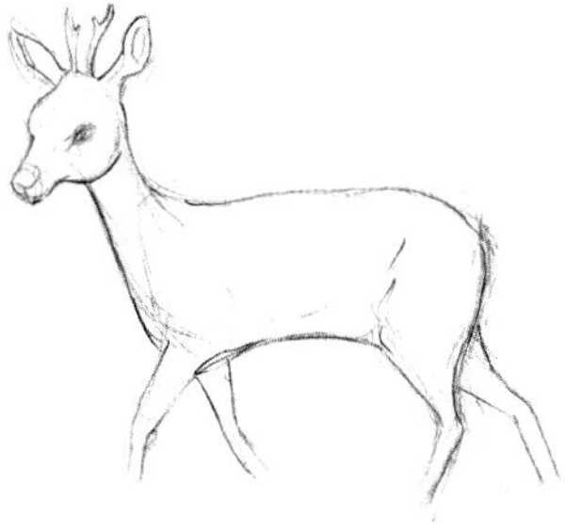

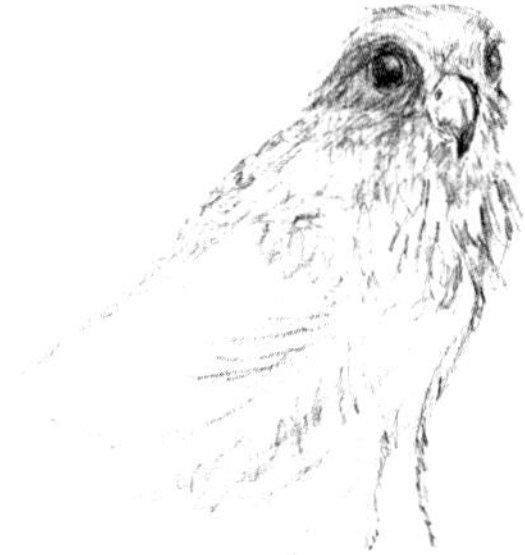

Leaving the fell, we were treated to the sight of a roe deer, gracefully trotting across the road in front of us, as we slowly descended off the fell through a heavily forested area.

A chance view of a kestrel on the ground, having caught its prey.

Creating more detailed studies in the studio allows me to explore anatomy further and to experiment with surfaces, trying to find different ways of communicating my experiences. This small drawing is graphite pencil on clayboard.

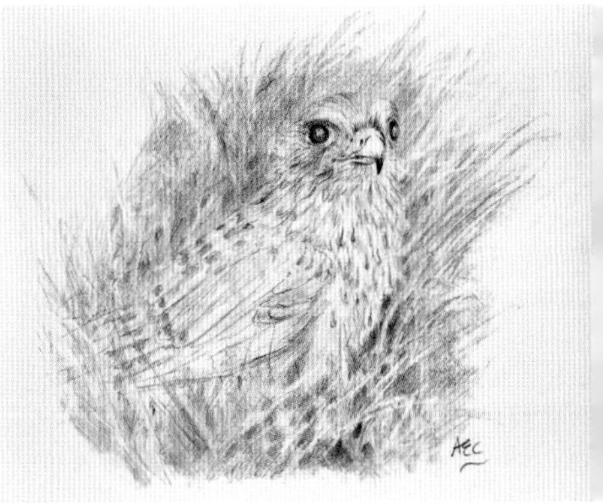

Rendering Details and Edges

The artwork here is of meadow buttercup flowers in Red Bay, Canada. The sea and sky were grayish blue, and like Saddle Island in the near distance, required little detail. Atmospheric perspective can be seen in the far distance. The harsh environment with rolling sea mists, even in summer, is at odds with the decorative yellow and gold of the flowers with their chaotic stem arrangements. It was tempting to add detail to every flower but that would have given the composition a static feel when there was constant movement. I implied this in the rendering of the flowers, by applying barely perceivable edges to some and high detail to others.

This drawing shows the complex design of the flowers and stems as they cross in front and behind each other, giving the impression of a pattern. When tone and detail is added, they appear more realistic.

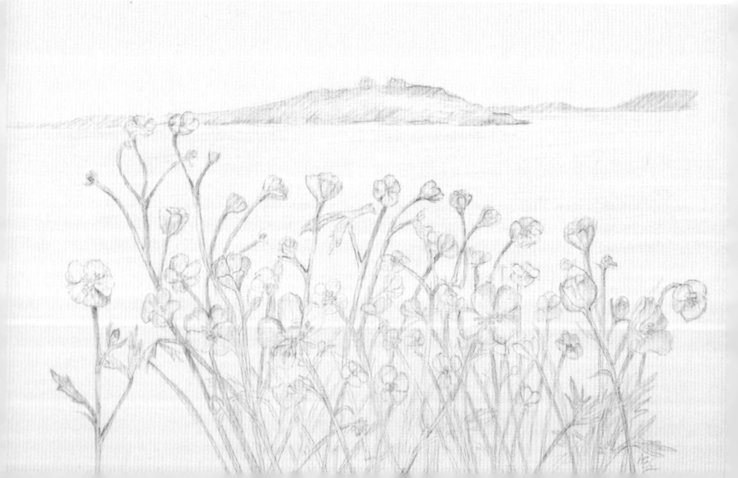

There are different ways to create and render art of botanical subjects. Botanical art is a specialist area where it is important to show accurately measured drawings and paintings of specimens, including their local color. Unless there is a need for a scientifically accurate illustration and labeling, you can use your own creative license.

When looking at multiple flowers and plants, I can only really see detail in those closest to me and in my line of sight. I draw in the same way, adding detail to some but not to others, which gives a more realistic feel to the drawing.

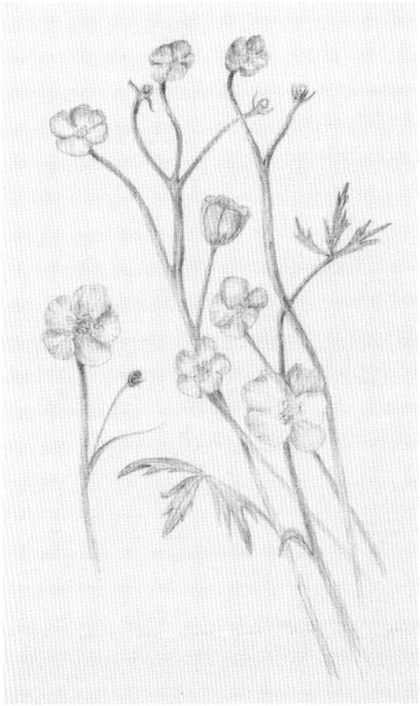

Using Shapes

When drawing animals, I try to find something unique to portray. Horses and ponies come in all shapes and sizes. A small shaggy haired pony is often easier to draw, as the shape is hidden under its coat, than an animal where the surface anatomy and contoured musculature is clearly defined, such as in a thoroughbred horse.

An understanding of what is under the surface is helpful here. Thoroughbred horses are built for speed with a streamlined body and long legs, devoid of muscle below the knee or hock joints. With such complex shapes and angles, it is tempting to only draw the horse at rest and to focus on the head and neck. I challenged myself to try and take the drawing further and to explore different poses and movement.

FINDING EXPRESSION

In a horse at rest, a keen expression with eyes wide and ears pricked forward, is enhanced by adding highlights to the eye and modeling to the face by applying shadow and highlights. A moving horse may have flared nostrils with visible veins apparent over the body. Drawing the hair as if it is being blown gives the impression of movement.

The aim of this sketch was to capture the intelligence of this thoroughbred horse, my own, from many years ago. A strong concentrated gaze and an interest in his surroundings show his inquisitive character.

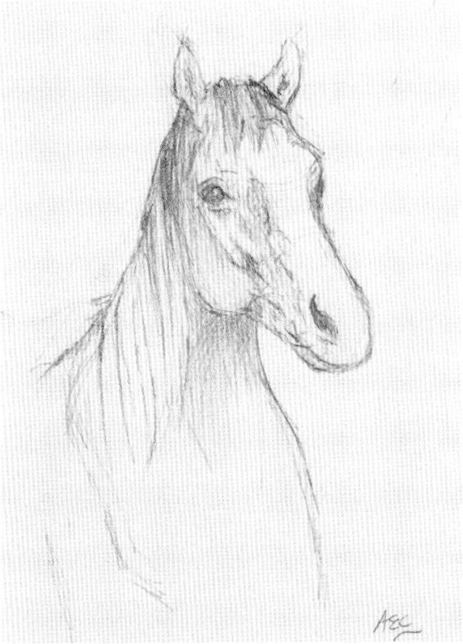

A thoroughbred horse is built for speed, so it makes sense to introduce movement in my drawings.

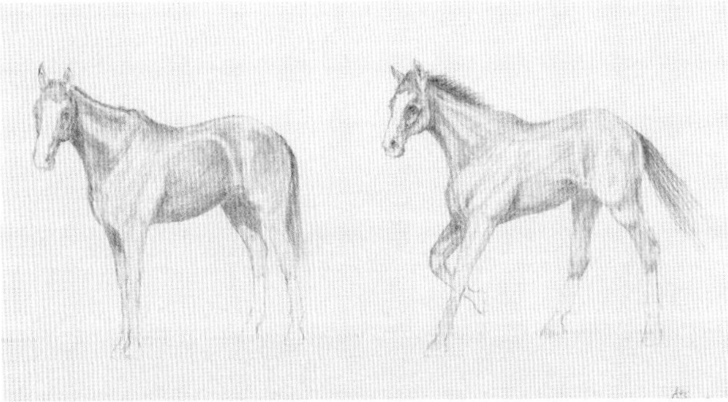

CHAPTER 10

Refine Your Drawing

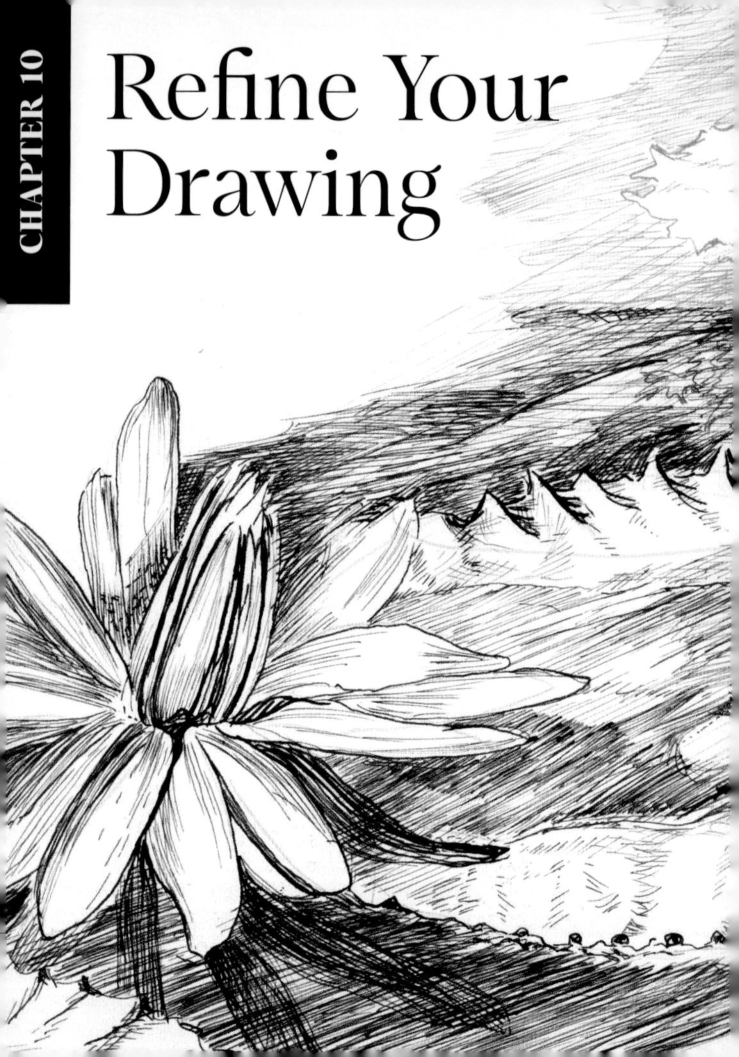

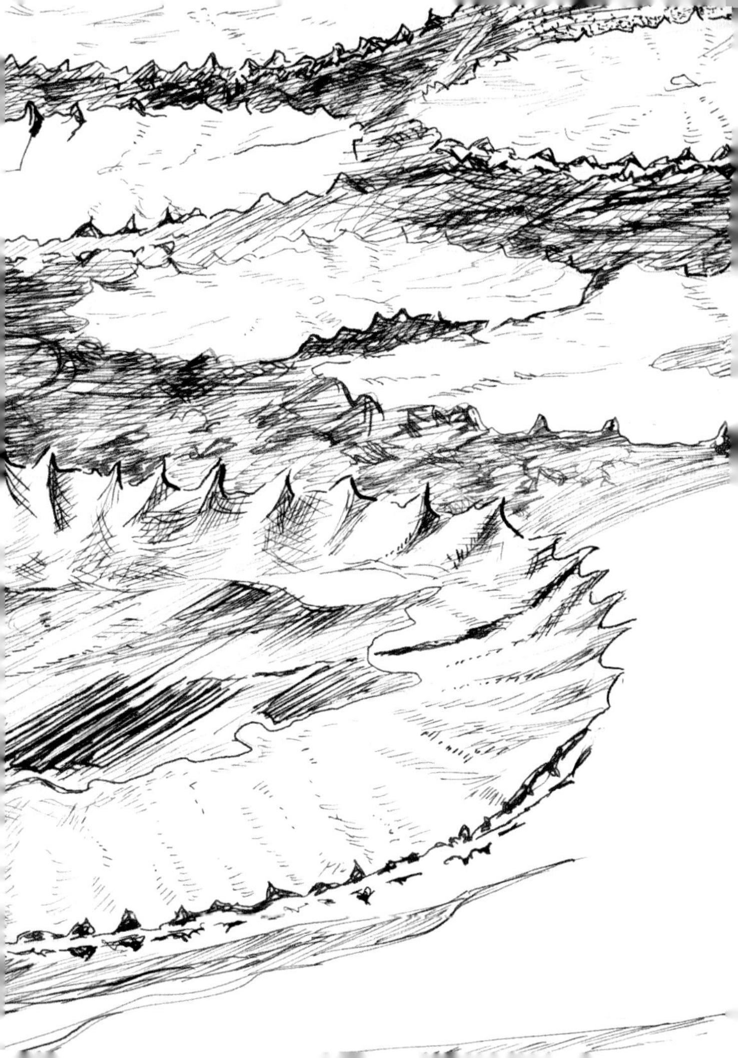

Finishing Touches

Learn to refine your artwork, as well as refining your life to make time for drawing. It is easy to think that you don't have time to be creative. However, think of that same creative moment of inspiration that got you making artwork in the first place, and it can actually become an integral part of life.

Using Your Skills

Refining your drawing means bringing into play all the creative skills you have developed. Planning, preparation, learning and practice, observation, recording, exploring options with research, decision making, designing, producing, and then being able to self critique and share your work are all part of the creative process that develops. These are all transferable skills that can be applied to other parts of life.

Being able to draw could help you on your pathway to a career in the creative arts. We've had a digital revolution so drawing can be done with a computer, even on a hand-held device. However, the humble pencil has not been lost along the way. Many working artists still prefer to work with a pencil, scanning work when the composition and preliminary artwork is complete.

Photograph your work as you progress. Develop creative and critical thinking. Film your work with your phone, talk to the camera, and learn how to talk about your artwork. These are all valuable ways to refine your artwork and your creative process.

As you develop your drawing skills, look back at earlier work and see how lines have become more refined and have purpose, how tonal values have gained more range and are more effective at describing form, how color is used both to interpret and inform, and how your artwork has narrative. Refining your artwork also means finding the final touches that will transform it into a good drawing—the addition of a subtle highlight or reflection, or a little more emphasis in a shadow area.

You can create finished artwork in a good-quality sketchbook—it doesn't have to be on a single sheet of paper. This line and watercolor wash piece is as significant as any other final artwork that I've created. It was drawn and painted on location on the Great Wall of China and, to me, that gives it huge relevance, even if it is in a sketchbook.

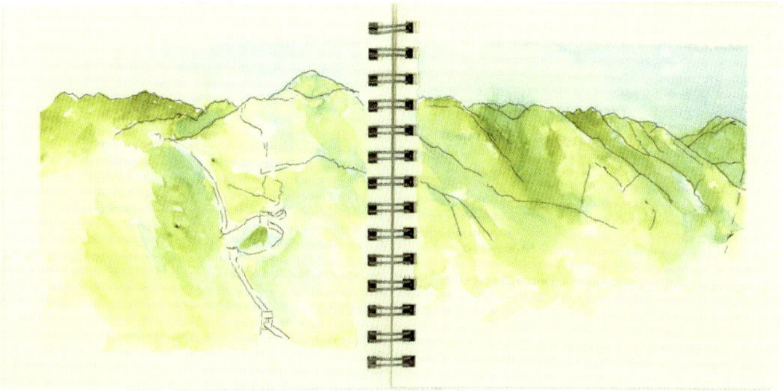

Develop a Sketchbook Drawing

With every drawing, I gain experience, which often makes me want to develop an artwork further. The original drawing of this scene on sketchbook paper worked out better than I expected. The only problem was, it was on two sheets of sketchbook paper.

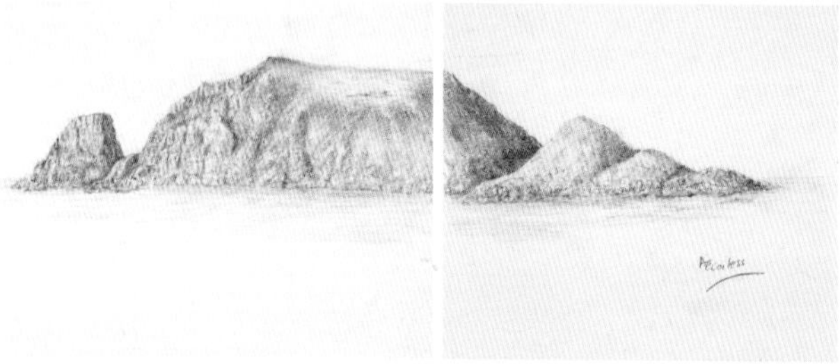

The original drawing of an island, on two sheets of sketch paper.

The aim was to build on the original composition by adding different elements. The island is in the background, so I could move it into the mid-plane or the foreground, but that would mean cropping it and it is the shape of the entire island that is dynamic. Fitting landscapes onto the drawing plane is often a challenge, so it is useful to find paper to fit the composition proportionally.

I then let my imagination take over! I added an eagle coming down to fish, and to the left of the island, is a blow of a whale, with the blow spreading across the horizon.

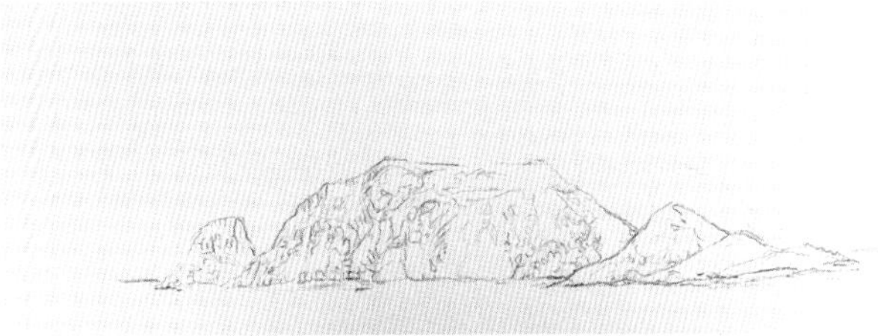

This sketch shows the detail necessary before applying value and more detail.

This is the final drawing, having used the original as a starting point.

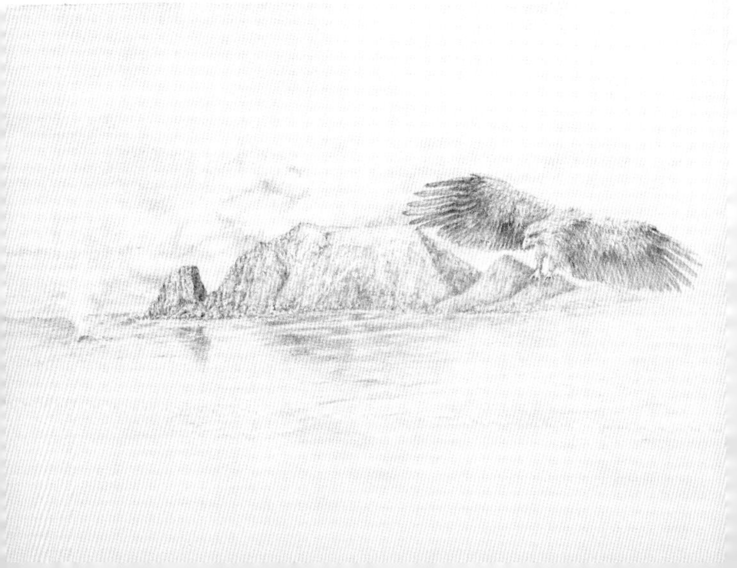

Refine How You Create Drawings

When looking for visual references to draw, it is usual to get one idea stuck in your head. However, try going back to the same photographs and sketches to create an entirely different, more detailed drawing from the same reference.

The lily pond was originally a pen drawing, an urban sketch. Thinking back I remembered seeing the beauty of the reflections and shadows and realized that I could create an entirely different drawing. I wanted to see how I could show soft edges on the lilies in the distance and detail on the lilies in the foreground, and emphasize shadows to show the beautiful reflections.

The final pen and ink drawing features hatching and cross hatching marks for shadow.

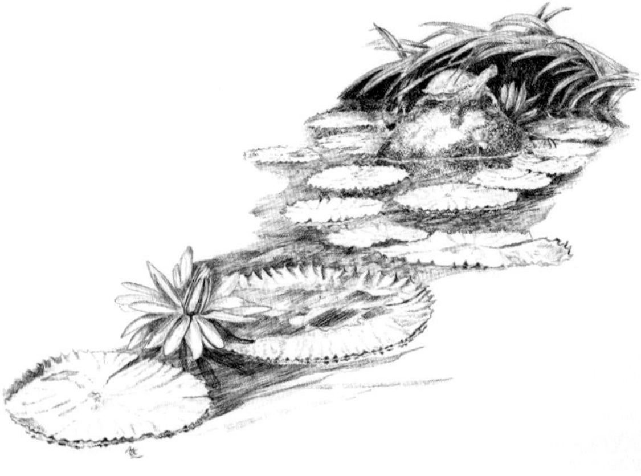

The water lilies with their large circular leaves and beautiful flowers arranged across the pond give almost limitless composition choices. My composition leads the eye from the dramatic flower and semi-submerged leaves to the turtle.

Preliminary drawings in pencil give a guide for the final artwork.

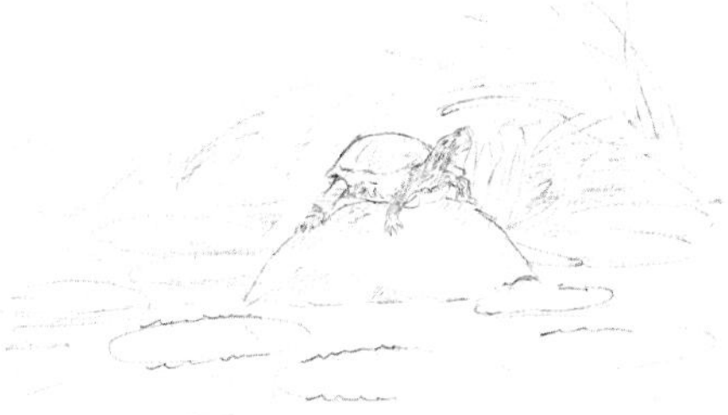

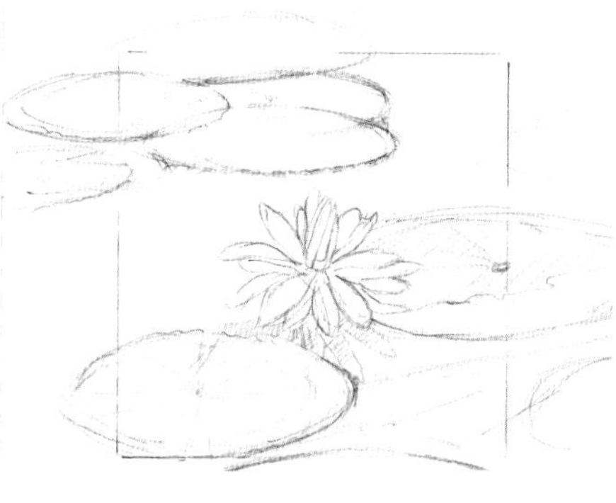

Making a Statement

Creative styles can be changed to suit a subject. Making decisions on how to render final artwork is part of refining your drawing skills.

In the preliminary drawing of this scarlet macaw (see Chapter 6), where the focus was on anatomy, it was easier to draw the bird more upright, whereas the actual angle of flight is seen here. With this final artwork, I focused on trying to create a dynamic image, showing the interplay of light on the feathers (colored pencil removed with a kneaded eraser to lift a highlight) and movement of different areas as the wings bend.

Macaws are often seen static and on perches but I wanted to show the heights they can reach in flight and so I suggested densely covered forest areas far below using light pencil marks. In this drawing, the bird is supported by air currents, the most natural position for it to be in.

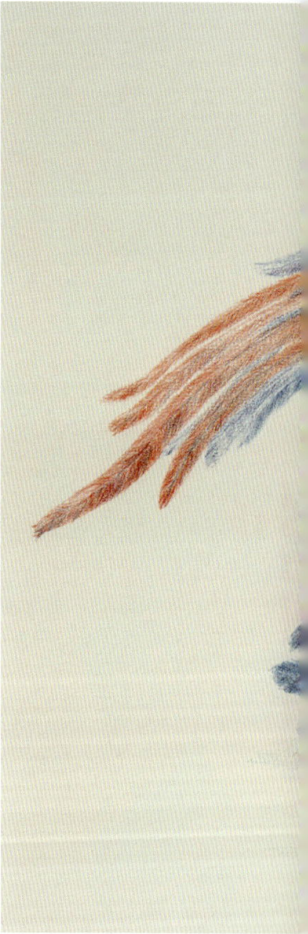

A landscape I saw years ago in Panama adds interest to this colored pencil drawing of a wild scarlet macaw.

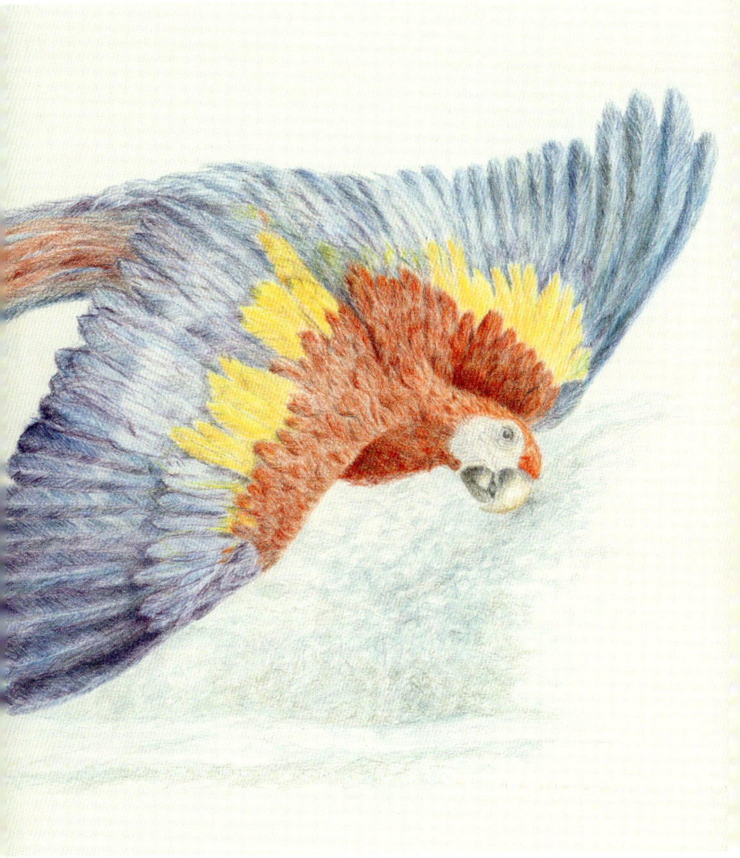

Completed Artwork

Is your artwork a personal project, for personal development or enjoyment? I know from experience that there are drawings and paintings I have produced that I will never part with as I have developed an emotional attachment to them. Drawing can become a means of expressing your feelings. Once basic skills are mastered, it will become your unique voice, responding to the world around you.

Farewell to a friend: a single stag stands, surveying his territory. This artwork is a homage to a friend, who introduced me to the magnificence of the natural world in the Scottish Highlands.

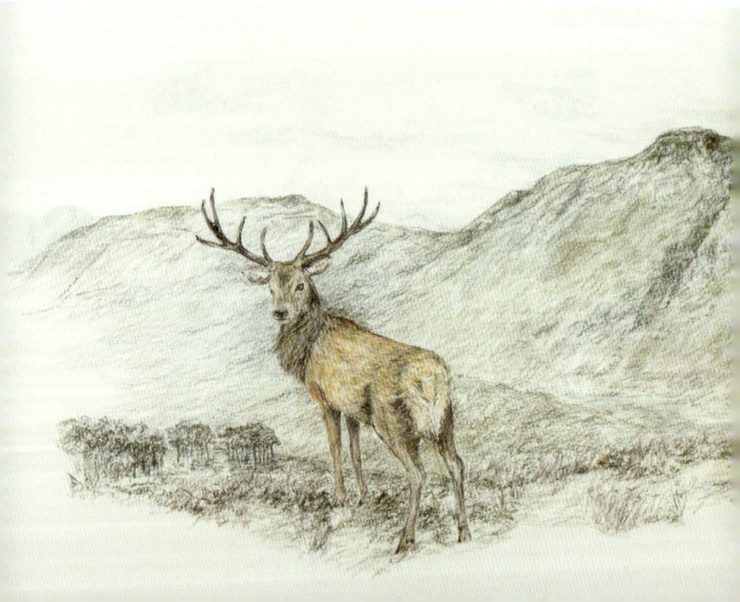

- If your aim is to sell your artwork, remember that art materials must be lightfast and long lasting. The next step is to learn basic business skills for artists, such as how to frame drawings, how to price artwork, and even how to make prints of your artwork.
- Protect artwork with acid-free archival sheets of paper and preferably store them flat, away from sunlight and moisture.
- Develop your record-keeping skills, making notes of art materials used, where you sourced references from, and the date the artwork was completed.
- Remember to sign your artwork!

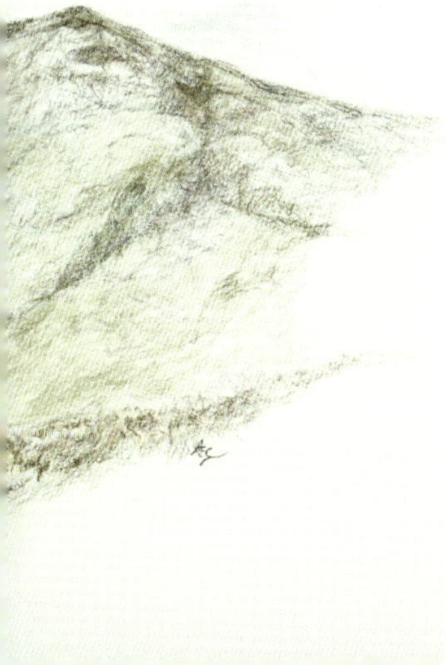

CAREER PATHS

There are many options for a career in the arts and a common theme is that the ability to draw is important, whether with traditional or digital media. These careers include: architect, character designer, concept artist, costume designer, fashion designer, illustrator, medical and bio-sciences artist, scenic artist, storyboard artist, and visual effects artist, to name a few.

About the Author

Based in Lancashire, England, Anne Corless has had a busy career in the creative arts, working as an artist, medical illustrator/multimedia designer, creative educator, and writer. Experienced with both traditional and digital media, Anne enjoys working in many areas of the creative arts.

Acknowledgments

I would like to thank the following for allowing me to create artwork of their plants and creatures: Blackpool Zoo, Gardens by the Bay (Singapore), and the Mandai Wildlife Reserve, Mandai Wildlife Group (Singapore), where I drew the Australian pelican, sacred ibis and scarlet macaw. Thank you to Featherbase (featherbase.info) for the information on the scarlet macaw feathers.

For all the friends we meet on our travels around the world, and especially to all our friends and colleagues at Fred. Olsen Cruise Lines, thank you for the years of encouragement, support and fun. You have all made it such a pleasure.

To my husband Bob, who shares my love of travel, the natural world, and photographing our travel adventures. Thanks for sharing it all with me and coping with "life with an artist." To my wonderful grown-up kids and their families, who have all learned how to cope with an artistic mum/mother-in-law, who is always wanting to go off to draw and paint. Thank you.

And lastly to my dearest mum, who was thrilled about this book, and who listened and mostly supported my madcap creative ideas over the last twenty years since we lost my dad... thank you for the fun and adventures. They meant the world to me.

INDEX

A DAVID AND CHARLES BOOK

David and Charles is an imprint of
David and Charles, Ltd
Suite A, Tourism House, Pynes Hill,
Exeter, EX2 5WS

EU GPSR Authorized Representative:
Logos Europe, 9 rue Nicolas Poussin,
17000, La Rochelle, France
Email: Contact@logoseurope.eu

First published in the UK and USA in 2026

A catalogue record for this book is available from the British Library.

ISBN-13: 9781446316955 hardback
ISBN-13: 9781446317075 EPUB

This book has been printed on paper from approved suppliers and made from pulp from sustainable sources.

FSC www.fsc.org MIX Paper | Supporting responsible forestry FSC® C020056

Printed in China through Asia Pacific Offset for: David and Charles, Ltd, Suite A, Tourism House, Pynes Hill, Exeter, EX2 5WS

10 9 8 7 6 5 4 3 2 1

Publishing Director: Ame Verso
Senior Commissioning Editor: Nigel Browning
Publishing Manager: Jeni Chown
Editor: Victoria Allen
Copy Editor: Clare Ashton
Lead Designer: Sam Staddon
Designer: Anna Wade
Pre-press Designer: Susan Reansbury
Production Manager: Beverley Richardson

David and Charles publishes high-quality books on a wide range of subjects. For more information visit www.davidandcharles.com.

Share your art with us on social media using #dandcbooks and follow us on Facebook and Instagram by searching for @dandcbooks.

Layout of the digital edition of this book may vary depending on reader hardware and display settings.